ASIAN ENTERP|

CW00517681

L.E. NIAMH's
GOODWILL VOYAGE
TO ASIA 2002

Edited by Brian O'Kane

·OAK·TREE·PRESS·

www.oaktreepress.com

OAK TREE PRESS
19 Rutland Street, Cork, Ireland
http://www.oaktreepress.com

© 2002 Oak Tree Press

A catalogue record of this book is
available from the British Library.

ISBN 1-86076-256-5 (paperback)
ISBN 1-86076-262-X (hardback)

Design and layout: Sean O'Leary
Cover based on "Asian Odyssey" by Irish artist Philip Gray,
The Philip Gray Gallery, Slipway Two,
Rushbrooke Commercial Park, Cobh, Co Cork, Ireland
Printed in Ireland by ColourBooks.

CONTENTS

A/S Gerard Dore, DSM

FOREWORD

The Government published "A Strategy for Long-term Development of Foreign Earnings in Asia" - the Asia Strategy - in December 1998. This document is a comprehensive review of Asia's long-term economic prospects, Ireland's interests there and our official representation in the area, and the critical issues in establishing a unified policy approach to Asia.

Given the planned visit of LE NIAMH to Eritrea in 2002, the Government recognised a unique opportunity for extending that voyage onwards to selected ports in Asia, highlighting the growing ties between Ireland and Asia. The partnership between three major Government Departments - Defence, Enterprise, Trade and Employment, and Foreign Affairs - along with the Naval Service and Enterprise Ireland, coupled with the enthusiastic support of the Irish business community and that of LE NIAMH's Captain, Lt Commander Gerard O'Flynn, and his crew, secured the success of a novel diplomatic, business and logistical initiative.

The visit came at a crucial time in the development of Ireland's relationship with the region. The Asia Strategy signalled the beginning of an intensive effort to build awareness of Ireland in Asia and to promote economic, trade and cultural ties. business and cultural efforts built around the visit of LE NIAMH illustrated the progress we have made in consolidating these links to date and helped to foster new relationships.

ASIAN ENTERPRISE: LE NIAMH's Goodwill Voyage to Asia 2002 provides a fascinating insight into the deployment of an Irish naval vessel on a multi-dimensional mission - one that by all measures was a resounding success. Our Departments and all those who were privileged to be associated with LE NIAMH's voyage to Asia in 2002 will long hold the memory of that remarkable and exciting endeavour. Our thanks and appreciation go to everyone involved, and particularly to the men and women of LE NIAMH.

Michael Smith, TD
Minister for Defence

Mary Harney, TD
Tánaiste & Minister for Enterprise, Trade & Employment

Brian Cowen, TD
Minister for Foreign Affairs

INTRODUCTION

ASIAN ENTERPRISE: LE NIAMH's Goodwill Voyage to Asia 2002 tells the story of a unique partnership between the Irish Navy, Enterprise Ireland (the State agency charged with promoting local Irish industry), Irish businesses and the Irish community in Asia, supported by the Irish embassies in the region.

Venturing further than any Irish naval vessel has ever been, LE NIAMH (LE stands for "Long Eireannach", Irish for "Irish ship") travelled 23,000 miles in 100 days, visited 14 ports (two of them twice), hosted over 10,000 visitors (including nearly 2,500 key business decision-makers) at over 60 functions, and represented 33 Irish companies and agencies.

A diplomatic, business and logistical success story, the credit for the success of this goodwill voyage and trade mission lies primarily with LE NIAMH's captain, Lt Commander Gerard O'Flynn, and the crew, who were in the front-line throughout. This book is foremost their story.

It is also the story of Ireland's burgeoning confidence and success in business, framed by the far-sightedness of the Government's Asia Pacific Strategy, the efforts of Enterprise Ireland and the many other State agencies and, in particular, Irish business men and women who seek opportunity in Asia. This book is their story too.

And last, this book is a tribute to the hospitality of the State and Local Government officials and their naval counterparts in the many countries LE NIAMH visited on her voyage.

LEFT, LE NIAMH berthed in Tokyo, Japan
RIGHT, Ready to receive guests onboard

THE VOYAGE

Under the command of Lt Commander Gerard O'Flynn, LE NIAMH departed Cork Harbour on a goodwill voyage to southeast Asia on Sunday, 10 February, beginning both the longest overseas mission undertaken by the Irish Navy as well as the largest trade exercise undertaken by Ireland in the Asia region.

The fraternity of the seas is universal, and "showing the flag" and "goodwill visits" by naval ships are major instruments of diplomacy internationally. The presence of a foreign naval ship in port creates an increased awareness of its country in the ports it visits. The ease with which naval personnel from different cultural backgrounds relate and interact is an important element of such diplomatic effort. The preliminary work undertaken by Embassies in planning a Naval visit also generates business and economic contact, which might not otherwise arise.

NIAMH's tasking on this voyage had a two-part mission:

• Supporting Irish Defence Force involvement in the UN Mission to Ethiopia and Eritrea (UNMEE)
• A goodwill visit and trade mission to Asian countries.

The voyage represented an operational and logistical challenge to Lt Commander O'Flynn and his ship's company, which consisted of 41 personnel, augmented by two different Cadet (trainee Officers) classes, and their training officers.

On departing Cork Harbour, NIAMH initially routed across the Mediterranean, making its first port of call at Valletta, capital of Malta and a fortified stronghold straddling ancient sea-routes.

Next, the ship made history by being the first Irish Navy vessel to transit the Suez Canal and into the Red Sea. There, it made an important re-supply call to the port of Massawa in Eritrea, in East Africa, where supplies and stores were delivered to and collected from the Irish troops serving with the UNMEE peacekeeping contingent. Massawa was also used as a fuelling stop, on the outward and return legs of the deployment.

After the next refuelling stop in Cochin, at the southern tip of India, LE NIAMH began the goodwill part of her voyage, hosting a large number of promotional events designed to support the export efforts of individual Irish companies and the work of the State development agencies. The aim was to attract 2,000 Asian business decision-makers onboard the ship to interact with Irish companies and agencies involved in Asia. The first stop was Singapore, followed in quick succession by Hong Kong, Shanghai, Incheon and Tokyo.

This part of this tasking, termed "Asia Deployment

2002" by the Navy, was a recognition by Government of the unique characteristics of Navy vessels for "furthering policy objectives in the international maritime domain" (White Paper on Defence, February 2000).

The voyage also formed part of the Government's Asia Pacific strategy, conducted in association with the Department of Foreign Affairs and Enterprise Ireland, which recognises the importance of the Asian market to Ireland.

For the single largest trade promotional event ever mounted by the State in Asia, NIAMH was used as a platform to raise awareness of Ireland, and to support promotional efforts by Enterprise Ireland, the Embassies, the other development agencies, and by individual Irish companies.

12,000 miles from home, NIAMH began her return journey on 15 April, heading for Penang, Malaysia, *en route* crossing the Equator, where its pioneering spirit met obstacles in keeping up old seafaring traditions. Penang was the last stop on the promotional tour.

Then it was homeward bound, retracing much of her outward route to Cochin, Massawa and Suez, with a Mediterranean stop at Palma, Mallorca. And finally, home at last on Tuesday, 21 May, with her mission complete.

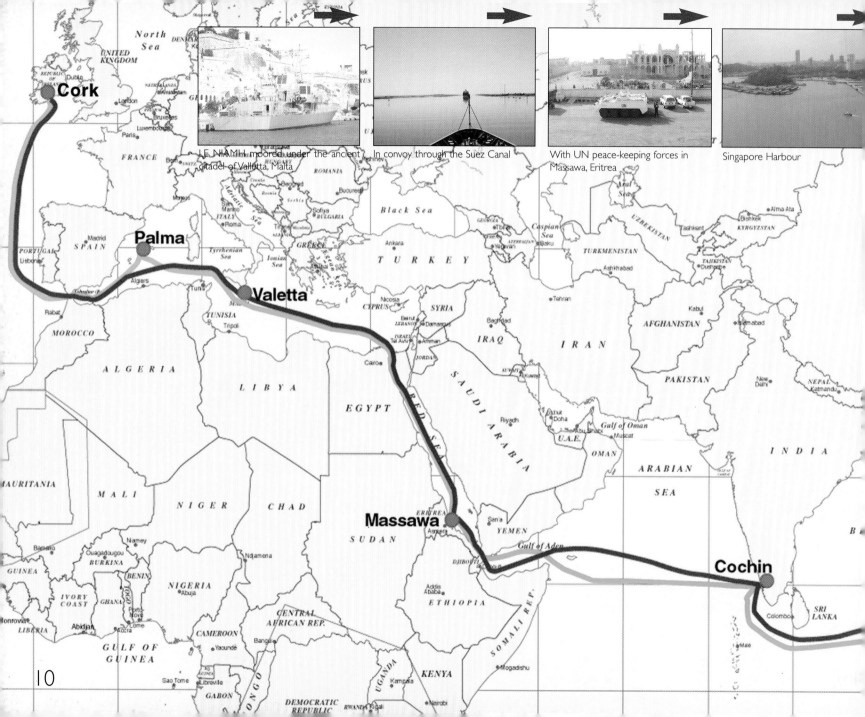

LE NIAMH moored under the ancient citadel of Valletta, Malta

In convoy through the Suez Canal

With UN peace-keeping forces in Massawa, Eritrea

Singapore Harbour

Cork

Palma

Valetta

Massawa

Cochin

g Kong at night

LE NIAMH at berth in Shanghai

Moored beside host ship DAECHON, Incheon, Korea

Imperial Palace, Tokyo

Traditional Temple, Penang, Malaysia

MONGOLIA

N. KOREA

Beijing

Sea of Japan

Pyongyang

Seoul

Inchon

S. KOREA

Yellow Sea

JAPAN

Tokyo

Tokyo

C H I N A

Shanghai

East China Sea

Taiwan (Formosa)

TROPIC OF CANCER

Hong Kong

MYANMAR (BURMA)

VIETNAM

Hanoi

LAOS

Vientiane

South

PHILIPPINE SEA

THAILAND

Bangkok

CAMBODIA

Phnom Penh

China

Manila

PHILIPPINES

ANDAMAN SEA

Gulf of Thailand

Sea

SULU SEA

Penang

M A L A Y S I A

Kuala Lumpur

CELEBES SEA

MALACCA STR

Singapore

EQUATOR

ASIA DEPLOYMENT 2002

CORK	DEPART, 10 February
Valletta, Malta	15 - 17 February
Suez Canal, Egypt	19 - 20 February
Massawa, Eritrea	23 - 23 February
Cochin, India	01 - 01 March
Singapore	07 - 11 March
Hong Kong	15 - 22 March
Shanghai, PRC	25 - 30 March
Incheon, Korea	01 - 04 April
Tokyo, Japan	08 - 15 April
Penang, Malaysia	24 - 28 April
Cochin, India	02 - 03 May
Massawa, Eritrea	08 - 09 May
Suez Canal, Egypt	11 - 12 May
Palma, Mallorca	16 - 18 May
CORK	RETURN, 21 May

WHERE IT ALL BEGAN

LE NIAMH's Asian voyage began in Dublin on a typical dull afternoon in February 2001. Peter Coyle, Executive Director of Enterprise Ireland, responsible *inter alia* for Ireland's trade promotion activities in Asia, was attending a meeting of the Irish Business and Employers Confederation's (IBEC) Asia Committee together with Joe Hayes, then the Assistant Secretary General at the Department of Foreign Affairs, responsible for Asia. Joe Hayes was "an old Asia hand", having previously been Ambassador to China (he is now Irish Ambassador to the Czech Republic). During a coffee break, the lack of Irish "profile" in Asia arose during casual conversation between the two men. Perhaps drawing on a successful Enterprise Ireland reception onboard the Irish Navy's flagship, LE EITHNE, in New York during the previous summer, Coyle and Hayes had a flash of inspiration: Why not send a Naval vessel on a promotional trip to Asia? They pored over the maps in Coyle's pocket diary and traced out there and then a route that would match remarkably the final voyage plan followed by LE NIAMH in 2002!

In the next few weeks, both men canvassed support within their own organisations. As a result, the Minister for Foreign Affairs, Brian Cowen TD, wrote to his colleague, the Minister for Defence, Michael Smith TD, seeking the use of a vessel for a promotional visit to Asia to raise Ireland's profile and, specifically, to promote Irish trade and Irish exporting companies. While Minister Smith and his officials considered this matter – which involved a significant financial outlay from their budget and the diversion from normal duties of a ship – other parts of the Government in Dublin began to come onboard the project.

An early supporter was Brian Whitney, the Assistant Secretary General at the Department of Enterprise, Trade and Employment, who chaired the Government's crucial Asia-Pacific Strategy Committee (APSC), which subsequently provided the funding for promotional events onboard NIAMH throughout Asia. APSC involves representatives of Government Departments and agencies, as well as private organisations involved in Asia (see separate panel on page 15 for more information).

Another important early supporter for the trip was Marie Cross, who succeeded Joe Hayes in Foreign Affairs. She quickly enrolled the enthusiastic support of the Irish Ambassadors throughout the region, while Peter Coyle of Enterprise Ireland did the same with Enterprise Ireland's representatives in Asia, who are led locally by Michael Garvey out of Hong Kong.

A key supporter for the voyage was the Navy's military "boss", Irish Defence Forces Chief of Staff, Lt General Colm Mangan. An internationally-minded soldier with

Peter D Coyle,
Executive Director - Asia,
Enterprise Ireland

Marie Cross,
Assistant Secretary,
Dept. of Foreign Affairs

extensive experience all over the world on United Nations peacekeeping operations, Mangan accurately foresaw that a successful voyage to Asia by NIAMH would not only benefit the Navy but would also have a beneficial effect on the overall image of the Irish Defence Forces and help them to recruit in Ireland's tight labour market.

A crucial turn in the political decision-making process came on 18 September 2001, when the Tánaiste (Deputy Prime Minister) and Minister for Enterprise, Trade & Employment, Mary Harney TD, flew with the Minister for Defence, Michael Smith TD, from Dublin to Cork on an Irish Army Air Corps Beechcraft Super King Air, to commission LE NIAMH. During the short air trip, the Tánaiste mentioned her Department's interest and support for a Navy voyage in Asia (Enterprise Ireland is an agency of the Department of Enterprise, Trade & Employment). Later that day, at a reception onboard NIAMH following her commissioning, an enthusiastic Minister Smith requested Peter Coyle of Enterprise Ireland to "… submit an economic case for this voyage immediately!".

Just before the commissioning ceremony, Peter Coyle was invited by NIAMH's Captain, Lt Commander Gerard O'Flynn, to visit the Officers', Senior Ratings' and Junior Ratings' Messes to outline the thinking that lay behind the possible voyage to Asia and the standards that would be expected from the crew. He recalls being so impressed by the sailors' positive reaction that he said to himself, "This team can do it. They can bring this small vessel to Asia and represent their country on a sustained basis at a very high level and do so with élan and excellence".

Of course, the Navy was not unaware of the discussions taking place between the various Ministers and Government bodies in Dublin and was already preparing contingency plans, led by Commander Mark Mellett, Staff Officer in charge of Policy and Plans at Navy Headquarters in Cork. In fact, the grapevine had been hard at work within the fleet and at the Naval Base at Haulbowline Island in Cork Harbour. The then Flag Officer Commanding the Naval Service (known to all as "the Flag"), Commodore John Kavanagh, later recounted with a twinkle in his eye how he had been offered a variety of Asian meals as he went from ship to ship during naval

LE NIAMH leading CIARA and ORLA on manoeuvres

manoeuvres in the latter part of 2001! Clearly, ships' captains were jockeying for the opportunity to sail to Asia.

However, officials at the Department of Defence, led by Secretary General David O'Callaghan, no doubt found themselves in a somewhat challenging position. On the one hand, they wished to be supportive of a major diplomatic and trade initiative but, at the same time, they had a reasonable concern about the impact on the Navy's other responsibilities of the departure from Ireland for an extended period of a patrol vessel. In time, this was addressed temporarily by stepping up the already high productivity of other vessels. Once the political "green light" was given to the voyage in late 2001, David O'Callaghan and Assistant Secretary General Michael Howard's team were very supportive and helped to expedite preparations for the voyage.

LEFT, Hong Kong harbour, looking towards Victoria Peak

ASIA PACIFIC STRATEGY

A Strategy for Long-Term Development of Foreign Earnings in Asia

December 1998

Department of Enterprise, Trade and Employment

A Strategy for Long-term Development of Foreign Earnings in Asia, popularly known as the "Asia Strategy" or "Asia-Pacific Strategy", was published in December 1998, prompted by the visit of the Taoiseach (Prime Minister) to China earlier that year. The Strategy is a comprehensive review of Asia's long-term economic prospects, Ireland's interest and official representation in the area, and the critical issues in establishing a unified policy approach to Asia. Recognising the long-term importance of Asia, the Strategy identified the low profile of Ireland in Asia as a major issue, and gave priority to raising awareness of Ireland in Asia, particularly in Japan and China, during the period up to 2004. An Asia-Pacific Strategy Committee ensures an integrated approach to the development of Irish ties in the region. It funded a sustained awareness-raising campaign, of which the visit of LE Niamh in 2002 was the most visible project, as well as new diplomatic and trade promotion facilities in Beijing, a new Irish Embassy in Singapore and new consulates in Sydney and Shanghai. Enterprise Ireland also boosted its resources in the area by establishing "incubator" facilities for Irish companies in Singapore, Shanghai, Tokyo and Beijing, moving its Regional Headquarters to Hong Kong and establishing a new office in Sydney to cover Australia and New Zealand.

PLANNING AND PREPARATION

Lt Commander Gerard O'Flynn,
Captain LE NIAMH

Onboard LE NIAMH, planning for the voyage began on 7 November 2001, the date on which official sanction of the deployment came through from the Department of Defence. The ship's Captain, Lt Commander Gerard O'Flynn, Marine Engineer Officer Lt Commander Michael Malone, and the Executive Officer Lt Owen Mullowney considered all aspects of the tasking. They prepared a detailed plan that identified who onboard was responsible for what and when and where it was to be done or provided.

Onshore, a Naval Base co-ordinating group was established by Commodore John Kavanagh (then Flag Officer Commanding the Naval Service), and led by Captain Frank Lynch (now Commodore Lynch).

A myriad of detail had to be considered in the planning process, from budgets for the deployment as a whole through to the printing of access and exit signs in the language of the various countries that were to be visited, from the scale and type of catering to be provided (including the provision of *Halal* foodstuffs where appropriate) to medical examinations and inoculations against a range of tropical diseases for all the crew. Not least in the planning was the need to arrange for the crew to be paid a portion of their salary in the various local currencies throughout the voyage.

NAVIGATION

The Navigation Officer, Lt Roberta O'Brien, drew up a detailed navigation plan. Calculation of accurate distances and speeds was of critical importance to ensure that arrival times for each port could be planned, and programmed into the detailed itinerary. In drawing up the plan, she had to research detailed information on tides, currents, and weather systems as well as the special rules applying to different seaways and ports and harbours. Fuelling arrangements had to be given special consideration, including accurate assessments of fuel consumption, and identification of fuelling stops. Fresh water did not pose a problem, as the ship manufactures its own fresh water from seawater using reverse osmosis.

The timing of NIAMH's transit of the Suez Canal had to be carefully planned, since ships transit the Canal as part of a convoy, of which there is only one per day in each direction. There were also many detailed administrative requirements to be met for each port - failure here could lead to delays and additional costs. The loss of even a single day would have caused havoc to the overall schedule. Fortunately, all went according to plan and when NIAMH anchored off Singapore on 6 March, she was 12 hours ahead of schedule - exactly the allowance that had been made in the plan!

ABOVE, Navigation Officer Lt Roberta O'Brien
BELOW, Petty Officer Cronan Doyle examining a weather fax
RIGHT, L/S Paul Patterson, O/S Siobhan Fennell, O/S Sharon Darby and
A/S Kevin Heade preparing for guests' arrival on board

CATERING

The ship's Supplies Officer, Senior Petty Officer, John Duffy, had to plan how to feed not only the crew for the four-month period of the voyage, but also the thousands of visitors who would be entertained onboard. Guest capacity had to be accurately assessed, so that whatever numbers were agreed could be comfortably catered for.

To ensure that, wherever possible, Irish cuisine would be served to guests, Bord Iascaigh Mhara (the Irish Fisheries Board) and Bord Bia (the Irish Food Board) supplied special stocks of Irish fish, beef, and cheeses sufficient to last the full deployment in specially-installed deep-freeze compartments. Irish companies - among them, Baileys, Blarney Mineral Waters (owned by Dairygold), Cooley Distilleries, Guinness, Heineken, the Irish Dairy Board, Irish Distillers, Kerry PLC, and Waterford-Wedgwood - supported the venture with their products. These Irish goods proved to be the subject of much

Cooks Alan Ferguson and Michael O'Keeffe

favourable comment for their fine quality.

CERT, the State body responsible for training in the hotel and catering sector, provided a special training course for the ship's catering staff, which significantly enhanced their confidence and planning capacity.

SECURITY

The ship's own security also had to be considered as part of the planning process. Although long thought to have been consigned to history books, maritime piracy has re-emerged as an issue of international concern. Documented piracy activities - many of them in the waters off south-east and south Asia - range from opportunist theft from ships at anchor, through more sophisticated attacks on ships on passage, to actual hijacking of ships. Worldwide, almost 2,500 piracy incidents were recorded in the period 1991-2001, although these figures probably understate the problem, as many incidents go unreported. All available information suggested that a Navy ship was unlikely to be the focus of such an attack. Notwithstanding this, NIAMH could not afford the risk of embarrassment and additional security measures were put in place when transiting higher risk areas.

UNDERSTANDING LOCAL CULTURES

Onboard NIAMH, the importance of understanding and respecting local culture, customs, and traditions was emphasised. Ainichi Ltd, a Dublin-based consultancy specialising in advice and services in relation to doing business in Asia and Japan, conducted a seminar on Asian culture & communications issues at the Naval Base prior to

departure. The seminar contributed significantly to a higher quality of service delivery, by giving the ship's company a greater cultural appreciation.

SHIP'S ORGANISATION

Given the extremely busy programme for the voyage, it was apparent from an early stage that successful function management would require the enthusiastic commitment of the whole ship's company.

It was also apparent that the traditional duty system of one day on/two days off would not be adequate to meet the standard of service delivery required. An alternative duty system was devised, based on a two days on/one day off system, involving the entire ship's company. This system, and a clear communication of the requirements of the tasking, empowered the ship's company and gave all the crew a sense of ownership of both the problems and solutions.

Business and military strategists are unanimous on the value and importance of a Mission Statement, in creating a driving force, direction and culture for any organisation. NIAMH's Mission Statement was redefined, based on a competition among the crew, held shortly after initial departure from Cork. The desire to embrace the role as ambassadors for Ireland, as well as derive some personal satisfaction, was the common theme of the many entries. Accordingly, selection of the final wording was a relatively simple task: *"To enjoy ourselves while projecting Ireland in a positive light at all times"*. This statement was displayed on the ship's notice boards for the duration of the deployment. It stood the test of time and provided the

Asian Odyssey, specially commissioned from Cork artist, Philip Gray

driver from which key objectives were derived.

GIFTS

In addition to ship's plaques and crests, the principal gift item was a stock of prints of a painting of the ship by Philip Gray, the renowned Cork-based artist, and himself ex-Navy. These were gift-wrapped in a specially designed box, containing an insert with details of the ship and its role. Other "off the shelf" Philip Gray gifts were also procured and, along with whiskey & Bailey's miniatures sponsored by their producers, ship's brochures and other promotional literature, were included in a gift bag presented to the ship's many guests. In addition, the Football Association of Ireland supplied a full Irish soccer kit, and the Irish Rugby Football Unit also supplied some merchandise.

CONCLUSION

For the ship's crew, the voyage exposed them to a unique challenge. No longer were they in a traditional out-of-sight tasking, conducted in the unique privacy of the open sea, but in a very public way seeking to generate an increased awareness of Ireland, in the most important developing world market.

Their primary task was to ensure that, through their navigation and technical skills, the voyage was successfully executed. Their secondary task was to ensure that the demands of the many stakeholders, agencies and advisers were combined to deliver a quality service. That they succeeded in both, recognised by all stakeholders, is in large measure due to the quality of the planning undertaken in the three months before departure.

NIAMH – THE ORIGIN OF THE NAME

All Irish Navy ships bear the names of famous Irish women, from history or mythology.

As construction neared completion, a national competition open to all secondary schools was run to choose the name for the ship. The winner was **Michael Kearney**, then a 14-year old student from Calasanctius College, Oranmore, County Galway. The following is Michael's winning submission for the competition.

"In Irish myth and folklore, there were three characters called Niamh. One, Niamh, the wife of Conall Cearnach, who became the mistress of Cuchulainn during the last period of his life. Two, Niamh, the daughter of Celtchainn, who married Conganchas Mac Daire, a warrior, whom no one could slay. She learned the secret of his invulnerability and told her father, who slayed Conganchas. Niamh then married the son of Concharbhar Mac Nessa, Cormac Cond Longes. The third and most popular legend is that of Niamh, the daughter of Manannan Mac Lir, who became the lover of Oisin, the son of Finn Mac Cumhal. It happened on a misty summer morning as Finn and Oisin with many companions were hunting on the shores of Loch Lena in Kerry. They saw a maiden with beautiful golden hair coming towards them, riding on a snow-white steed. She wore the garb of a queen and the horse had golden hoofs and a crest of gold nodded on its head. When she came near, she said, 'My name is Niamh of the Golden hair, I am the daughter of the King of the Land of the Youth'. She asked Oisin to go with her to her father's land. Enchanted by her beauty, he agreed. They mounted her steed and rode towards the sea. When the couple reached the sea, the horse ran over the water, just skimming the waves as the green woods of Erin disappeared into the distance. They passed many wonders on the journey, including a golden boat. They had many adventures in the Land of the Youth and had three children. But, after what seemed to him only three weeks, he longed to visit his native land and to see his old comrades. He promised Niamh that he would return and she gave him the white fairy steed but warned that, if he set foot on his homeland, he would not be able to return to the Land of the Youth. When Oisin reached Erin, he met some men on a road trying to move some rocks. When he bent over to help, his saddle girth broke and he fell to the ground. He instantly turned into an old man and it is said he related his story of the Fianna and Niamh Chinn Oir to Saint Patrick before he died."

LE NIAMH's crest shows the three crowns of Munster, traditionally believed to be where the fabled Tir na nOg (Land of Youth) was located, as well as Niamh and her white steed.

NIAMH's crest was designed by Mrs Mary O'Brien, wife of the late Lt Commander Sean O'Brien, who designed all of the other current Irish Navy crests. Lt Commander O'Brien was the Irish Naval Historian and a story-teller of note.

STRATEGIC OPERATIONAL AND TACTICAL PLANNING

Commander Mark Mellett,
Plans and Policy Unit,
Naval Headquarters

STRATEGIC PLANNING

From a planning side, the strategic nature of the Asian 2002 deployment was recognised from the outset. Clearly, it was in the national interest that the deployment should be successful in all its aims. Initially, these aims were primarily economic and diplomatic in nature; however, very soon, a cultural dimension began to develop as the Irish community in Asia recognised the opportunity that the ship offered as a mobile Irish "centre of gravity" in the region. And, of course, the opportunity to carry out a military re-supply in support of Irish troops serving with the United Nations in Eritrea added another dimension. The cross-cutting forum of the Asia-Pacific Strategy Committee, with the temporary addition of Anne O'Neill of the Department of Defence and two officers (myself and Lt Commander Jim Shalloo) from the Plans and Policy Unit of Naval Headquarters, provided a mechanism to overview the strategic aspects of the deployment.

OPERATIONAL PLANNING

Operational decision requirements began with the identification of the most suitable ship to undertake the deployment. Only two options existed: The proven capacity of the LE EITHNE, which had already crossed the Atlantic on three occasions, or the untested LE NIAMH, whose futuristic lines had the potential to add significantly in portraying Ireland as a progressive technology-driven country. Having considered all issues, Commodore Kavanagh decided on the LE NIAMH. Once this decision was made, a significant number of minor, yet time-consuming, preparations had to be carried out on the ship.

With the support of the Naval Dockyard in Haulbowline, access ladders, safety railings and awnings were added to the onboard main reception area (on the part of the ship known as the Flag deck), so that best use could be made of the space for guest access and catering support. The awnings were later modified in Singapore through the intervention of Enterprise Ireland's Tokyo representative, Declan Collins, who was concerned about the cooler temperatures that would be experienced in Tokyo. He designed plastic side walls, which meant that the area could be fully enclosed without obstructing the views - an important factor when these included such world-renowned landmarks as the Rainbow Bridge in Tokyo, the Oriental Pearl Tower in Shanghai, and the Hong Kong Conference and Exhibition Centre. This timely intervention by Declan was typical of the positive working relationship that developed between Enterprise Ireland and the Navy.

From an operational perspective, it was equally

important to identify the most suitable weather window for the deployment - when the risk of tropical storms was least. This was why the deployment was timed for the early part of the year, rather than to coincide with the World Cup football matches, as some would have wished!

TACTICAL PLANNING

At a tactical level, there was a requirement to acquire up-to-date meteorological information, as well as port information on all the ports to be visited. With no historical data to rely on in terms of berths and services available in the target ports, we made contact through the Department of Foreign Affairs with the appropriate Naval authorities to ask for port information and recommendations on berthage. In addition, I was fortunate to be able to call on Naval colleagues in Singapore, South Korea and Malaysia.

Nonetheless, the complexity of the deployment was such that advance visits to Asian ports were required to draw up detailed programmes that integrated all the requirements of the various stakeholders. Lt Commander Jim Shalloo and I separately visited in advance all the Asian ports that NIAMH would visit prior to the ship's departure from Ireland, and met with the various agencies in each port. This ensured that the most suitable berths were procured, and that Enterprise Ireland and Department of Foreign Affairs representatives were properly briefed. Local handling agents were appointed, responsible for provision of ship services in each port, including berthing arrangements, pilotages, fuel delivery, etc. These visits were also important in establishing the various national protocols for visiting warships, as well as making informal contacts with ex-patriate Irish and supportive local nationals living in the target ports, which proved crucial in breaking through the bureaucratic issues that arose from time to time.

LE NIAMH, Singapore, as dusk falls

JOIN THE NAVY
AND SEE THE WORLD

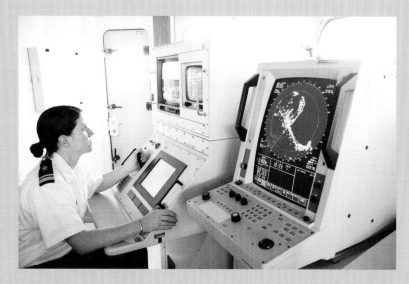

Navigation Officer Lt Roberta O'Brien operating the Integrated Surveillance System with the ship's Radar Display to the right

Join the Navy and see the world! When people said this to me, I always replied that, with the exception of one visit to Lebanon on a re-supply mission, my seagoing experience was confined to 200 miles off the coast of Ireland.

I was commissioned in September 1997, after a two-year cadet-ship. I graduated from the National University of Ireland, Galway in 2000 with a Bachelor of Science degree. In the Spring of 2001, I qualified as a Watch-keeping Officer and was approached by Lt Cdr Gerard O'Flynn (whose appointment as captain of LE NIAMH had been announced) and asked if I would be interested in joining the newest ship of the fleet as Navigation and Communications officer. I was thrilled to get such a fantastic opportunity. I would be setting up the two departments from scratch. What a challenge!

On completion of her sea-trials, NIAMH began her first patrol in July 2001. Four months later, just as I was settling into the routine of Navigation and Communications officer, I was told that the ship was being sent on an Asian deployment. No other ship in the Irish Navy had gone east of the Suez Canal before. I was really looking forward to the challenge. My responsibility as Navigation officer was going to be huge – I would be the first Irish Navy Navigation Officer to plan a passage of such magnitude.

The Captain briefed me on the outline plan. Hong Kong was identified as a focal point of the deployment, given that we were to be there for Ireland's National Day, St Patrick's Day. Distance and transit times between each port had to be calculated. Prevailing weather conditions had to be considered. In consultation with the Captain and Marine Engineering Officer, projected average fuel consumption was estimated, and the various fuel stops were identified. Thus we went from a general concept to a specific plan, with times of arrival and departure identified for each port. This plan was then forwarded to the various authorities that had to make specific arrangements, ranging from the Department of Foreign Affairs organising diplomatic clearance to appointment of agents in each port and ordering of specific fuel amounts.

Petty Officer Cronan Doyle compiled a very concise communications plan. This plan incorporated a list of reporting stations for traffic choke-points like the Suez Canal and Singapore Straits, sources of weather forecasts, harbour contact details and pilot stations, phone call costs for the different countries, high frequency (HF) and satellite communications plans, etc.

After consulting the numerous pilot books that describe the type of weather sea conditions, tidal effects, currents and traffic around the world, I began to plot courses on charts. A course is a pencil line on a chart delineating the ship's intended route. The courses were plotted on small-scale charts first and then transferred to more detailed large-scale charts. An electronic back-up known as ECDIS – Electronic Chart Display System – supported this manual system and proved to be a major labour-saving device, enabling me with the click of a button to make alterations and modifications to courses, to calculate distances quickly, to switch between charts, or to cross-check the paper charts with the electronic charts.

Having transited the Suez Canal, experienced beautiful sunsets, navigated through large concentrations of fishing vessels at night and into the busiest ports of the world, shopped in Singapore, swum at the Equator, and bargained in the markets of Shanghai, it is difficult to single out the best part of the deployment. However, being onboard NIAMH in Hong Kong Harbour on St. Patrick's Day is a memory I will always cherish.

How many people of my age get such an opportunity to travel around Asia? Most people pay to do this or, like a lot of my friends, take career breaks. I was getting to do this as part of my job! The best way to see the world? Join the Navy!

Street market, Hong Kong

BUILDING LE NIAMH

Lt Commander Michael Malone,
Marine Engineering Officer,
LE NIAMH

Lt Commander Michael Malone supervised the construction of LE NIAMH and has served as the ship's Marine Engineering Officer since her construction. He recalls the pleasure of the most exciting challenge any marine engineer could face.

In March 2000, following the signing of the contract to build LE NIAMH, I was tasked by Capt. Frank Troy, the then Marine Engineering Superintendent of the Navy, to act as Resident Engineer at Appledore Shipbuilders, Devon, England, supervising the construction project. Completion and delivery was set for September 2001.

At the time I had over 18 years' service in the Navy, as a Marine Engineer. I had acquired considerable experience drawing up detailed specifications for major refits and dockyard work for all the different classes of vessels in the Navy. By July 2000, the ship's side plates had been cut and numbered rather like a jigsaw, before being transported to the fabrication shop where the individual plates are welded using a metal inert gas process to form individual units or sections of the ship's hull. On completion of the units, a steel inspector engaged by the Navy, the classification society surveyor, and myself inspected all welds on the units. The units were then combined into larger blocks weighing up to 40 tonnes, prior to being lowered into the covered dry-dock where the vessel was built. The covered dock ensured that the build could proceed regardless of the weather. NIAMH was built by Appledore Shipbuilders, but

all electrical work, pipe fabrication, joinery, ventilation systems and communications installation were sub-contracted.

Other tasks included attending factory acceptance trials of various plant and equipment, including main engines and generators. The main engines were trialed on test beds in the Netherlands in mid-December and delivered to the yard in Christmas week 2000. An important milestone was reached in early January 2001, when the engines were lowered into the ship – an impressive sight and a real sign of progress!

NIAMH was floated out of the covered dock on Saturday, 10 February 2001 and moved to the fitting-out berth. Here, most of the piping, vent trunking for the heating ventilation and air conditioning, electrical cables, and ancillary engine room equipment were fitted. The joinery shop was close by and, towards the end of the build, the furniture was fitted. As and when each of the individual systems were completed, the system was commissioned – that is, inspected and tested to full working state.

Although six months ahead of the original schedule, the final stages of completion of the ship were absolutely hectic, with everyone concerned with the project working long hours and weekends. NIAMH departed Appledore in April 2001 to commence an extensive programme of sea trials and inspections, with Falmouth as the base. Additional members of the crew began to join the ship as the trials progressed. Following a final dry-docking, the project team accepted the ship on behalf of the State and, on 18 July 2001, the ship sailed with its first crew for Cork. Less than one week later, NIAMH was an operational Naval ship.

The opportunity to supervise the build of a new ship is one of the most exciting challenges that any Marine Engineer can experience, and I certainly relished it. I knew I would serve on the ship for the first two years of its operation but nobody told me that, within six months of operation, we would undertake a 23,000-mile round-trip to Asia. I consider myself extremely fortunate to have been part of a hard-working and technically competent ship's company on NIAMH who met every challenge with determination and energy.

LE NIAMH

TECHNICAL SPECIFICATIONS

Length Overall	78.84 metres
Beam	14.00 metres
Draught	3.80 metres
Displacement	1,500 tonnes
Speed	23 knots
Endurance at 15 knots	6,000 nm
Complement	44 (6 Officers)
Main Machinery	2 X Twin 16 cyl V26 Wartsila 26 Medium Speed Diesel giving 5000 Kw at 1000 RPM, 2 Shafts, 3 Caterpillar generators (420 Kw each) and a Volda bow-thruster (340 Kw)
Weapons	1 X 76mm Oto Melara (multi-purpose gun as main armament); 2 X .5" HMG (heavy machine-gun); 4 X GPMG (general-purpose machine-gun); 2 X 57mm Illuminating Rocket Launchers
Commissioned	18 September 2001

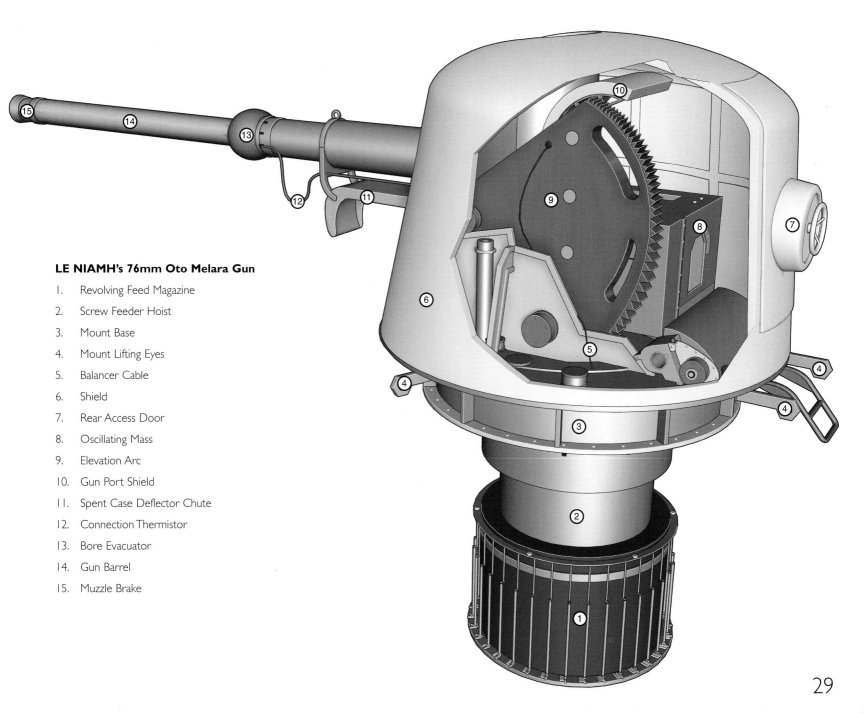

LE NIAMH's 76mm Oto Melara Gun

1. Revolving Feed Magazine
2. Screw Feeder Hoist
3. Mount Base
4. Mount Lifting Eyes
5. Balancer Cable
6. Shield
7. Rear Access Door
8. Oscillating Mass
9. Elevation Arc
10. Gun Port Shield
11. Spent Case Deflector Chute
12. Connection Thermistor
13. Bore Evacuator
14. Gun Barrel
15. Muzzle Brake

LE NIAMH exterior

1. Petroleum Storage Jettison Rack
2. Starboard Rudder
3. Starboard Propeller
4. Effer Crane
5. GPMG (General Purpose Machine Gun)
6. 5.4 m RIB (Rigid Inflatable Boat)
7. Accommodation Ladder
8. Inter Ship Gangway
9. Pyrotechnics Lockers
10. Satellite Communications and TV Antenna
11. Life Rafts
12. 6.8m (R.I.B) Rigid Inflatable Boat
13. Caley Davit (Single Point Lift)
14. Bilge Keel
15. Funnel with Engine and Generator Exhausts
16. Starboard Stabiliser
17. 0.5" HMG (Heavy Machine Gun)
18. Flag Deck
19. Main Masts with Radar and Communications Antenna
20. RADAMEC Optronic Surveillance/ Fire Control System
21. Searchlights
22. Starboard Navigation Light
23. 76mm OTO Melara Gun
24. Bow Thruster
25. Anchor Windless

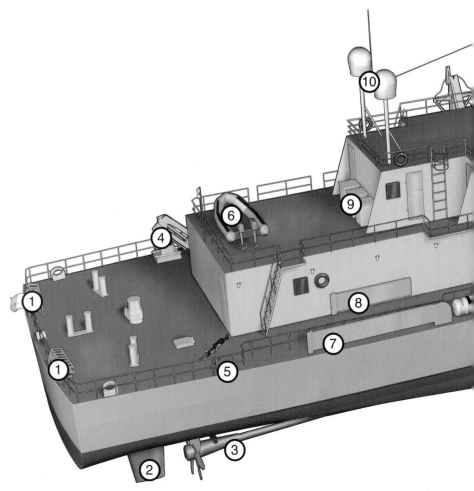

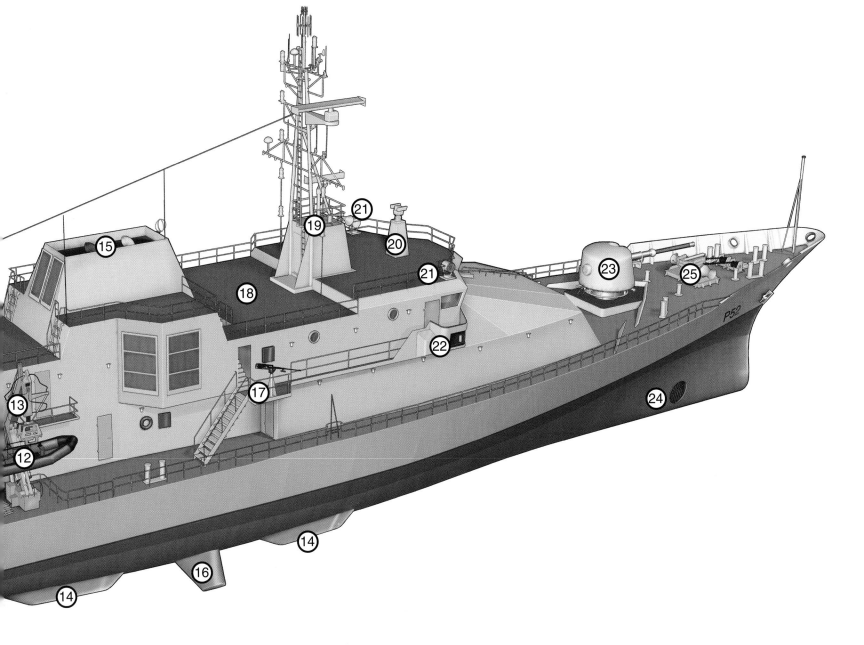

P52

LE NIAMH interior

1. Rope Store
2. Steering Gear Compartment
3. Divers Workshop and Changing Room
4. Food Store and Walk-in Fridge/Freezer
5. Laundry
6. Galley
7. Sick Bay
8. Senior Rates Mess
9. Exercise Room
10. Starboard Main Engine
11. Engine Control Room
12. Captains Cabin
13. Senior Rates Bathroom
14. Radio Room
15. Officer and Senior Rates Accomodation
16. Junior Rates Accomodation
17. Bridge
18. Senior Rates Accomodation
19. 76mm OTO Melara Gun

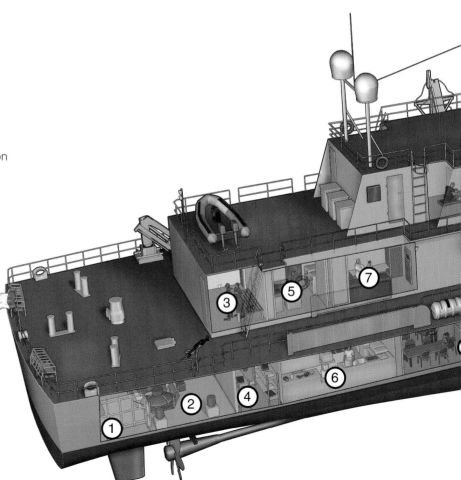

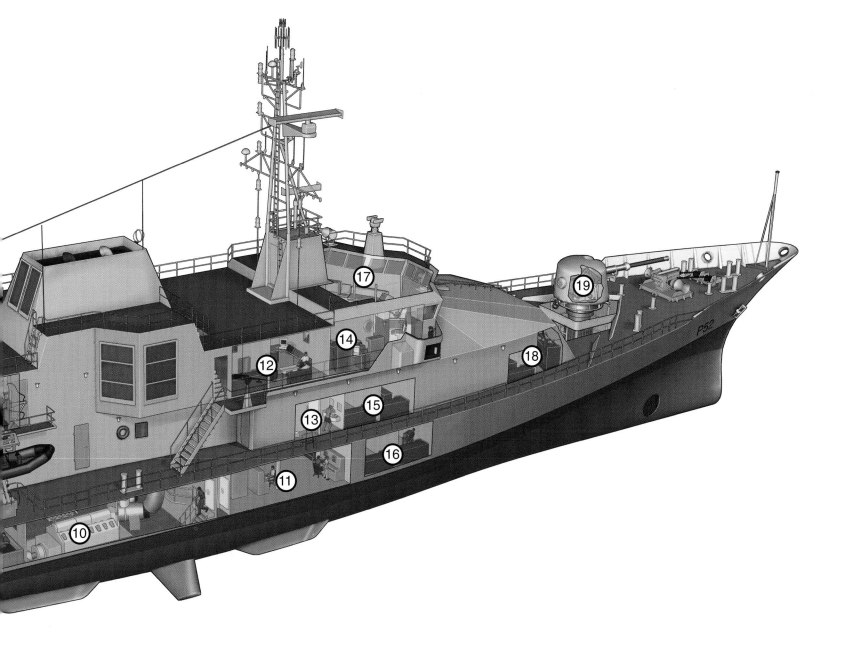

BON VOYAGE!

NIAMH's departure from Haulbowline Naval Base was a low-key affair, on a stormy February Sunday morning. As she slipped from Cork harbour through the rain, Flag Officer Commanding Naval Service, Commodore John Kavanagh, stood in silent salute on the Visual Signalling tower at the Naval Base.

However, only a few weeks earlier, at the height of preparations for the voyage, NIAMH had been honoured by a visit from the President, HE Mary McAleese and her husband, Dr Martin McAleese.

Speaking to the crew, the President said: "Your voyage to Asia is remarkable in many ways. It is the longest and most complex overseas deployment ever undertaken by the Navy. The ship will host a large number of promotional events designed to raise the profile of Ireland and to support the promotional efforts of both individual Irish companies and the State development agencies."

The President commented on the unique sovereign status of Irish naval vessels under international law, saying that "the ship will in fact equate to a piece of Irish territory in the sea areas and countries that it will visit".

She also pointed to the unique diplomatic nature of the deployment. Goodwill visits by naval ships are a major instrument of diplomacy, as the presence of a foreign naval ship in port creates an increased awareness of the country of its origin. In NIAMH's case, the fact that this would be the first Irish naval vessel ever to enter Asian waters added to the significance of its presence. Asia Deployment 2002 represented a recognition by the Government of the diplomatic potential of the Navy and gave practical recognition to the use of the Navy in furthering policy objectives in the international maritime domain.

The President and Dr McAleese then took time out to meet and talk with individual crew members, wishing them all "bon voyage!".

Flag Officer Commodore John Kavanagh watches LE NIAMH depart on her historic voyage

ABOVE: S/Lt Roberta O'Brien, Lt Commander Gerard O'Flynn, Captain LE NIAMH, Lt General Colm Mangan, Chief of Staff Irish Defence Forces, HE President of Ireland, Mary McAleese, Col PB O'Reilly, ADC to the President, Dr Martin McAleese, Commodore John Kavanagh, Flag Officer Commanding Naval Service

HAULBOWLINE TO SUEZ

Lt Owen Mullowney,
Executive Officer, LE NIAMH

The run from Haulbowline to Port Said on the Mediterranean coast of Egypt passed off smoothly, despite poor weather during the first few days. A brief stop at Valletta, capital of Malta, provided a break and then it was eastward again.

On Wednesday, 20 February 2002, nine days out of Haulbowline, NIAMH became the first Irish Navy ship to transit the Suez Canal. The canal runs from Port Said on the Mediterranean Sea for 87.6 miles to the Port of Suez on the Red Sea. Effectively, it links East and West – the Atlantic Ocean with the Indian Ocean. One of the most important shipping routes in the world, the canal was built in 1869 by manual labour under the direction of a French engineer, Ferdinand De Lesseps, who later worked on construction of the Panama Canal.

The canal has a capacity of 80 ships per day. A one-way system operates whereby traffic is organised into two daily convoys – one going north and the other going south. The convoys meet mid-way, at an area known as the Great Bitter Lakes. Here, one convoy anchors, providing space for the other to continue on its passage.

As a south-bound ship, NIAMH anchored off Port Said on the afternoon of 19 February. The ship's appointed agent boarded the ship and finalised the administrative tasks, which included checking its Suez Canal tonnage certificate, certificate of registry, and various other documents. Later that night, the local port control assigned the ship its place in the convoy and its departure time.

NIAMH got underway at 0200, when the first pilot boarded the ship. The pilot's job was to provide "local knowledge" to the Captain on how best to enter the canal. On entering the canal, the first changeover of pilots took place, along with the arrival of three boatmen and two electricians – each in a separate boat. The boatmen's job was to tend any ship's ropes or berthing lines in the event of the ship having to berth anywhere along the canal. Such a situation could arise if a ship developed mechanical difficulties – since this would require all following ships to stop, canal officials understandably are keen to take precautions to prevent or minimize such situations. The need for local personnel arises from the Egyptian authorities' unwillingness to allow unauthorised ships' personnel to land on Egyptian territory along the canal. The electricians fitted and tended a large searchlight to assist the ship's officers in guiding the ship through the canal at night. It took a little while for the new arrivals to set up their equipment and settle into their assigned overnight accommodation. The next morning, the electricians and boatmen set up their own little bazaar on the after deck, selling a variety of Egyptian souvenirs. Much enjoyable bargaining took place!

As the sun rose on a beautiful clear morning, the raw

beauty of the desert was seen for the first time. For much of the passage, all that could be seen were the banks of sand deposited on either side when the canal was dug, with frequent glimpses of the flat desert to the west over Egypt and the arid mountains and desert to the east over Sinai. Such a sight is truly unique and beautiful to sailors used to the very different beauty of the west coast of Ireland.

There was a further change of pilot at Ismail, just before the midpoint of the canal. The ship then entered the Great Bitter Lakes, where it is normal to anchor and await the passing of the north-bound convoy. However, NIAMH's pilot managed to negotiate a move from sixth in the convoy to second, which meant there was no need to anchor, thus much reducing the ship's transit time. Apparently, it is quite normal for warships to receive this special treatment. From the Bitter Lakes onwards, there was a noticeable increase in military presence along the banks of the canal, reminding NIAMH's crew of the canal's strategic importance and history of conflict.

At the Port of Suez, NIAMH again changed pilots and bid farewell to the friendly electricians and boatmen, all now sporting Irish Navy baseball caps. Here, the final pilot boarded, whose job was to provide navigation advice as the ship departed the canal for the Red Sea – as one crew member put it, "Another day, another sea". Thus ended the first transit of the Suez Canal by an Irish Navy ship.

LEFT, an impromptu bazaar on board LE NIAMH
NEXT PAGE, transiting the Suez Canal in convoy

MASSAWA, ERITREA

The final phase of the voyage from the Suez Canal to Massawa in Eritrea includes waters that require precise navigation. Soundings, or water depths, can change over a short distance from depths of several hundred metres to less than 30 metres. David Fleming, a second year Naval Cadet, recounts his experience during part of the passage through these waters.

"The time is 2359 and I am just coming on watch as the understudy Officer of the Watch. We are on a southerly course towards Eritrea. I am on watch with the ship's Navigation Officer, Lt Roberta O'Brien, and already we have had to alter course and speed to overtake other vessels. We have another vessel off our port bow travelling at 10 knots, which will have to be overtaken as well.

"The approaches to Massawa are very tight with islets and reefs close to our course, making the navigator's job very challenging. At least every 15 minutes, I take a fix by radar, measuring the distance between our position and at least three known points on land. Using a compass, these three ranges or distances are marked as arcs on the navigation chart (map) – their point of intersection is our position at that time. I also take visual bearings of lights or conspicuous land objects as an alternative means of establishing the ship's position. It is important to use the different means available to ensure that all systems are functioning properly."

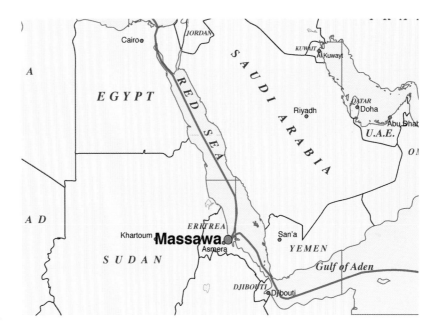

EXPERIENCING THE EFFECTS OF WAR FIRST HAND, FIRST TIME - MASSAWA, ERITREA

Cadet Dominic Kelly

Unloading supplies for UNMEE Forces

On Saturday, 23 February, NIAMH berthed in Massawa in Eritrea in order to offload supplies to the Irish troops serving there with the UNMEE Force (United Nations Mission in Ethiopia and Eritrea). Eritrea is a country covering an area of 121,320 sq. km, with a population of 3.8 million. It has a troubled history, having emerged from a war with its neighbour, Ethiopia. While in Massawa, **Cadet Dominic Kelly** spent a few hours exploring the city. Here, he outlines his impressions.

"We arrived in Massawa just after 0730 (local time) and picked up our pilot at the entrance to the harbour. Our pilot, a former naval officer, was there to provide local navigation information and berthing details so that our Captain could safely navigate the ship into the harbour. The pilot was a professional and friendly person, a trait that we were to observe as being common to the Eritrean people. In fact, many of the Irish troops compared the people in Eritrea to the Irish in their friendly nature.

"We tied up at a prime berth right beside the gates to the harbour, directly across from what was once a palatial building, but is now a mere shell of a building after heavy aerial bombardment. Waiting on the quay wall was a warm welcome from the members of the Irish contingent of the UNMEE force, some of whom were familiar faces from the Irish Navy, including Senior Petty Officer John Kearney, Leading Seaman Jim Morrisey, Leading Radio Radar Technician Paul Brophy, Medical Technician Aiden Mernin, Chef Brendan Fitzgerald, Telegraphist Stewart Hamilton, and Supply Assistant Brendan Cassidy. The Irish troops are in Eritrea as part of a UN Mission to monitor a ceasefire in place since June 2000.

"After supplies and ammunition were offloaded to the Irish convoy, our colleagues from the Army were good enough to provide a briefing on the MOWAG Armoured Personal Carrier. They also provided a guided tour of Massawa. Travelling around the hot Eritrean town seeing all the destroyed buildings felt like being on the set of "Black Hawk Down". I saw the innocent victims of war first-hand, some of them living in small huts constructed from cut branches, cut-up grain sacks and corrugated iron. Located in a prime location in Massawa town is a war memorial consisting of three tanks on elevated marble

platforms that were captured from the Ethiopian Army – in contrast to their previous use, their gun barrels now fire only water.

"Eritrea is a country that has potential to become a popular tourist destination in a few years' time. It has some reasonable hotels at very affordable prices and a very friendly population. There is much to see here including magnificent scenery and beautiful beaches. The crystal clear water was just what was needed to cool off from the 30-degree plus temperatures in the midday sun.

"It was great to meet the Irish troops who had been in Eritrea for the previous three months, especially several of our Naval colleagues, as well as soldiers from my home town of Drogheda.

"It was an experience of a lifetime to visit a war-torn country and to see first-hand the suffering experienced by people living in such horrendous conditions, the consequence of a prolonged conflict. We all hope UNMEE will help this country rebuild itself. Overall, I was both impressed and saddened by what I saw in Massawa, but I took great pride in seeing Irish troops help restore peace to a part of the world that has suffered for too long."

41

COCHIN, INDIA

Lt Cathal Power, Cadet Training Officer, LE NIAMH

Cochin (also known as Kochi) is situated in the province of Kerala, on the southwestern tip of the Indian subcontinent, with the Arabian Sea to the west (known locally as the Lakshadweep Sea) and the Western Ghats mountain range to the east. The dense tropical forests, extensive peaks and ravines of the Western Ghats have sheltered the province from invaders over the centuries. They have also encouraged maritime contact with the outside world, from which the city of Cochin has grown and prospered. Today, Cochin is a thriving commercial port, home to the Indian Navy's main training facility, and a population of over 12 million people.

Lt Cathal Power is the Training Officer for the 40th Naval Cadet class, who were embarked on NIAMH. An appointment as a Class Training Officer is normally of two years' duration, and is a much sought-after appointment amongst Operation Branch Officers. Along with his class, Cathal joined NIAMH in Cork on 10 February and remained onboard until the ship arrived in Hong Kong. Here he recounts his experience of the ship's visit to Cochin, India.

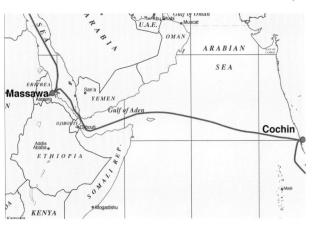

"We were due to arrive at Cochin on Friday, 1 March. By Thursday evening, we had sufficient time in hand to include a swim in the Arabian Sea. The ship heaved to (stopped at sea) for 'Swimming Stations' 260 nautical miles west of the Indian coastline. Some people claimed that swimming in the Arabian Sea was an even more enjoyable experience than the Red Sea, and this time nobody was bitten by pesky jellyfish! The water was even warmer – a comfortable 27 degrees Celsius. After our dip in the Arabian Sea, we continued towards Cochin. Later that evening, we encountered three Indian Naval ships, and a Naval helicopter exercising in the area. They later approached us to carry out a Visual Flashing Exercise, during which we exchanged international call-signs. In the unspoken bond between sailors at sea, they welcomed us to India and Cochin, and wished us a safe and successful voyage for the remainder of our deployment.

"We planned to arrive in Cochin at 0800 local time. The 'Morning Watch' (0400 – 0800) on the bridge were monitoring the ship's progress very closely when, just after sunrise, the ship's radars suddenly came alive with literally hundreds of contacts. Out of the morning haze appeared Cochin's local fishing fleet. This fleet of small 20-foot open deck boats sat en masse, 10 miles off the coast, forming a near impenetrable barrier to the Indian coastline. NIAMH had quite a task maneuvering through the fleet, which seemed oblivious to any of the large vessels in the area, continuing on its centuries-old trade of harvesting the seas.

"As we entered the approach channel to Cochin Harbour, the pilot and an Indian Naval liaison officer boarded NIAMH. Full ceremonial honours were rendered to the Naval officer, the first Indian liaison officer ever to board an Irish Navy ship. The officer was dressed in 'full whites', complete with sword and scabbard – the full ceremonial summer uniform (No. 1s) worn by many navies operating in the Tropics. The pilot was dressed less formally in shorts and short-sleeved shirt – though still 'all white'.

"Through the morning haze, we entered Cochin harbour, with Fort Cochin and its famous fishing nets passing along our starboard side. Nearing our berth on Willingdon Island in Cochin harbour, we could already see that local traders had set up shop on the quay wall, vying for space with each other.

"Among the dignitaries who had come to welcome NIAMH was Patrick Scullion, Deputy Chief of Mission at the Irish Embassy in New Delhi, who had co-ordinated the advance planning, including berthing arrangements, provision of fueling and supplies. Thanks to his diligence, everything that had been planned for Cochin ran smoothly.

"He was definitely a most welcome sight for another

reason! We were due to receive mail, which he was carrying for us. Although most probably old news, there was still a rush to see who had received letters from friends and loved ones at home. Unfortunately, his mail-bag also included lots of official correspondence – plenty of work for some. Mr. Scullion also delivered the Referendum postal ballot papers for the whole crew. Although we were thousands of miles from home, we had an entitlement to vote.

"Once we were alongside, the Indian Navy's Protocol

Traditional fishing nets on the shores of Cochin

Republic of India

- Population: 1,029,991,145 (July 2001)
- Capital: New Delhi
- Port Visited by NIAMH: Cochin
- Irish Ambassador: HE Philip McDonagh
- Enterprise Ireland representative: Nick Marmion (based in Dubai)
- Enterprise Ireland clients active in India include:
  Acra Controls Ltd, Baltimore Technologies, Cement Roadstone Holdings, Dublin Business School, Griffith College, Inflight Audio Ltd, Institute of Education/Portobello College, PARC Aviation Ltd, Royal College of Surgeons in Ireland, Shabra Plastics & Packaging Ltd, Shanahan Engineering Ltd, SIFCO Turbine Components Ltd, SmartForce Ireland Ltd, Trinity Biotech Manufacturing Ltd, Western Automation R&D Ltd.

Visit – Key Facts:
- Number of functions: 1
- Number of visiting decision-makers: 14
- Total number of visitors: 70

NOTE: Cochin was a re-fueling stop on both legs. NIAMH hosted a reception for local Irish interests on the return leg of the journey.

Officer boarded with full ceremonial, which entailed the Officer of the Day (OOD) and Captain meeting him at the gangway of the ship, where he was 'piped' onboard by the Seaman standing by the gangway.

"Our appointed agent, who was to be our point of contact for all our fuelling and storing requirements, also accompanied the Protocol Officer. Re-fuelling commenced almost immediately. That day, there was a strike in Cochin due to the current political problems in other parts of India, but this had no effect on the fuelling and storing of NIAMH, all completed in a most efficient manner. At the berth, we were provided with phone lines and an Internet connection, our first since leaving Ireland in February.

"An Indian Roman Catholic priest, Fr Raja Reddy, also visited NIAMH in Cochin. He has many friends in Ireland, and they had organised and collected clothing for his organisation – 'Care for Helpless, Homeless, Orphaned Children and Aged' – which had been carried to India on NIAMH. He had travelled over 900 miles from Cuddapah to the north – a journey that took him nearly 24 hours by road, a short journey by Indian standards! It was well worthwhile to see the excitement and pleasure on his face as we offloaded his supplies. This donation meant that Fr Raja could redirect some of his funds to other projects, including cottages for the 300 children in his care. Glimpses of the world like this only make us realise how well-off we are in Ireland. [NIAMH's crew were so taken with Fr Raja's work that, on their own initiative, they organised a collection among themselves and made a further donation of clothing and goods on the return voyage. Editor]

"As is customary with visiting Naval ships, the Captain went ashore to make his Calls of Protocol. These are official visits by the Captain of the ship to the local dignitaries and to the senior Naval officer in the area, in this case Flag Officer Commander-in-Chief Southern Naval Command, Vice Admiral Singh. A tour of the Naval facility was organised for the embarked Naval Cadets. The Cochin Base is the Indian Navy's main training facility, and has a staff and student population of over 10,000. It also contains an important Naval dockyard.

"With a population of over 12 million, the city of Cochin has a very mixed culture, due to the fact it was subject to rule by a number of different European nations, down through the ages. The influence of Portuguese, Dutch and English cultures are very evident, making for a remarkable blend with the traditional Indian culture of the city. Cochin has many remarkable sights to visit, including the tombstone of Vasco Da Gama, the first European to reach India by sailing around the Cape of Good Hope on the southern tip of Africa, who died here in 1524. He was buried here for 14 years, until his remains were eventually returned to his native country of Portugal.

At 1700, with all the crew back onboard, NIAMH slipped and exited Cochin harbour through the evening haze. As we cleared the port, the Officer of the Watch (OOW) was again kept busy, as the ship transited through the Cochin fishing fleet. Even into the early hours of the following morning, NIAMH continued to encounter tiny open-decked fishing vessels, many of which were over 40 miles offshore in pretty fresh winds."

PO/ERA Stephen Bruton and LE NIAMH's port main engine

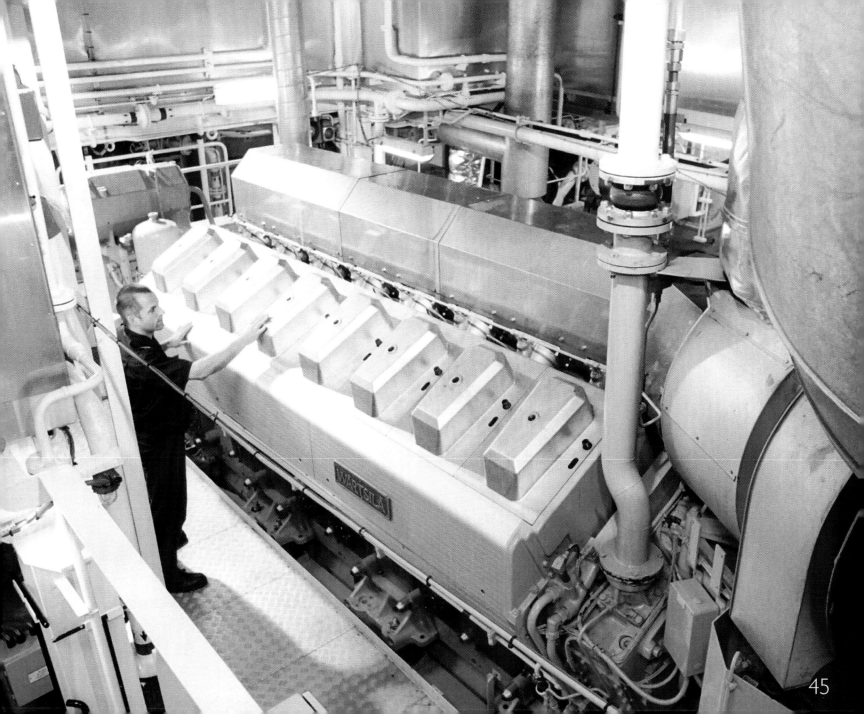

THE IRISH TRADE MISSION

关系
GUAN XI

Irish Navy vessels have made many trips abroad. The most important visit was to the US in 2000 when the flagship LE EITHNE visited a number of ports, including New York, where an International Naval Review was held. Quite frequently, vessels visit ports in the UK and in Europe and, of course, the Navy has visited the Lebanon on about 30 occasions over the past 20+ years in support of the Irish Army's involvement in United Nations peacekeeping activities there. None of these voyages, however, compared in duration, cost, complexity or ambition to the visit by LE NIAMH to Asia. So why did the many arms of the Irish Government come together to plan and execute a voyage which was, by any previous standards, one of immense logistical complexity?

ECONOMIC BACKGROUND

Asia is rapidly growing in importance to Irish-owned industry, the domain of Enterprise Ireland. Irish firms exported €1,147 million to Asia in 2001, driven principally by the Irish software industry. The growth of the software industry in Ireland has been the subject of endless fascination to Asian countries such as Singapore and China, which have sent numerous delegations to Ireland to study this industry. Irish companies now have 110 representative offices in Asia and the Mid-East region, compared to 28 offices as recently as 1998.

POLICY BACKGROUND

The Asia-Pacific Strategy Report (see page 15) stated that "... the 21st century is destined to become the 'Asian Century' ... Asia will account for one half of world trade by 2015".

The report went on to say that "... it is essential to increase the current levels of investment in developing political and economic relations with Asia, so that our Irish enterprise does not miss out on the market growth opportunities that Asia will provide in the long-term".

Most telling of all, the report states baldly that "... Ireland starts from a significant disadvantage in comparison with many of our competitors ... despite being active for over a quarter-century in Asia, Ireland still remains virtually unknown to the vast majority of people there ... many Asians who know anything at all about Ireland have a confused impression, assuming that we are part of the UK or even that we are Iceland ... This awareness problem arises because, historically, Ireland has had little political or economic contact with Asian countries. This legacy leaves Ireland in a very unfamiliar position: without either friendly networks or a positive image. It means that we face unique challenges in building relationships in Asia to promote an understanding about our competitive strengths as either a supplier of goods and services or as a location for Asian investment in Europe."

Finally, the report recommended that Japan and China be the major focus for Irish efforts for the period 1999 - 2004 and suggested that a promotional campaign be undertaken to raise awareness of Ireland among key decision-takers in Asia as a priority.

PROPOSAL FOR A VISIT BY A NAVY VESSEL

The Minister for Foreign Affairs wrote to the Minister for Defence in June 2001 proposing a visit by a Naval vessel to Asia. The intention was to use the vessel as a platform to raise awareness of Ireland in the area and to support promotional efforts by the Department of Foreign Affairs, Enterprise Ireland, other development agencies and individual companies. The proposal was widely welcomed across both the public and the private sectors and enjoyed support from groups as diverse as the Irish Business and Employers' Confederation and Irish-based English language training schools, represented by the organisation MEI-RELSA, who are active in seeking customers from Asia for their schools. In its submission, Enterprise Ireland stated that the proposed visit was "... one of the few tools immediately available to us to help Irish companies to raise their profile in Asia, to access clients and, ultimately, to close deals and safeguard jobs".

OBJECTIVE OF VISIT

It was agreed that the overall objective of the visit was to get 2,000 key Asian decision-takers - particularly in the business field - to visit the vessel and meet with Irish companies and agencies during the visit. It was stated also that, if this goal was attained, it would represent one of the most important ever awareness-raising exercises by Ireland in Asia and it would have a positive medium-term impact on exports and jobs.

THE TRADE MISSION

Doing business in Asia calls for an understanding of the various races, cultures and business practices in each country. An underlying assumption is that you do business with those you know – the corollary being that you know those you do business with – and, consequently, much time is spent in developing and "romancing" business relationships. The Chinese even have a special character called "Guan Xi", that symbolises the power of relationships.

The visit of LE NIAMH offered Ireland and Irish exporters a special opportunity to reciprocate the hospitality that Asian businesses, Government Ministries and Local Authorities provide in the normal course of business to Enterprise Ireland clients and their customers. Much of Enterprise Ireland's planning went into ensuring all key people were invited to the various functions hosted onboard LE NIAMH during the seven stop-overs in the course of the trade mission.

In the end, 33 Irish companies and agencies were represented on the Trade Mission, with 16 of these hosting specific functions on the ship. In addition, in each port, a general business and diplomatic function was organised and hosted the Irish Ambassador to that country. The chapters that follow tell the story of the trade mission, as LE NIAMH brought her "little piece of Ireland" to the far reaches of the world.

Companies and Agencies that took part in the Trade Mission onboard LE NIAMH included:
- AEP Systems
- Baltimore Technologies
- BIM
- Bord Bia
- Cork Language Centre
- DATAC Control International Ltd
- ESBI
- FreightWatch
- IDA Ireland
- Intuition Publishing
- Iona Technologies
- Kentz
- Linguviva
- MEI-RELSA
- Ocean West
- Shanahan Engineering
- Tourism Ireland

Other Irish companies and organisations that attended the receptions or events on board included:
- Eurologic
- Irish Business Forum
- Royal College of Surgeons in Ireland
- SmartForce

MEI-RELSA schools that participated included:
- Alpha College of English
- Atlantic Language Galway
- Cork English College
- Emerald Cultural Institute
- Galway Cultural Institute
- International House Icon
- Kenilworth Language Institute
- Limerick Language Centre
- Pace Language Institute
- University of Limerick Language Centre

21ST BIRTHDAY AT SEA

Victoria Kelly is a communication specialist onboard NIAMH. By rank and specialisation, she is referred to as a A/Com Op. She is Australian-born, having moved to Ireland in 1992 to live in Castlecomer, Co. Kilkenny. Here, she outlines how she came to celebrate her 21st birthday onboard LE NIAMH on 7 March.

"There is a long line of military service in my family – starting with my great-grand father, who served with the ANZACs against the Turks in Gallipoli. At present, my brother is serving with the Irish Army. So, when it came to my turn to choose a career, I looked to the Navy.

"Having enlisted on 6 December 1999, on completion of basic recruit training, I was assigned to the Communications Branch. After initial communications training, I went out onto the high seas in November 2000 on board the LE EMER. It was here I got my first real taste of life in the Navy and of the west coast of Ireland during winter!

"Last December, as the crew of NIAMH started their preparations for Asia Deployment 2002, I heard that they were short of a Telegraphist, my specialisation. It sounded like an ideal opportunity but I never thought I had a chance of being considered. With a little under four weeks before the departure date, I was still on EMER and about to head off on a well-earned spot of leave, when I got the word 'You're going to China'. I quickly found out that not only was the ship going to China, it was also going to Japan,

Korea, Singapore, and Malaysia – and that the deployment would coincide with my 21st birthday.

"Suddenly, it was a case of moving my kit to NIAMH, getting some leave to say goodbye to my family, sorting out credit cards and buying sun-screen, summer clothes and lots of camera film! Two weeks to go and I finally began my time on NIAMH. I'd met the Captain, who looked very familiar – I soon realised that he was none other than the officer who had interviewed me for my recruitment.

"On 6 March, we were anchored off Singapore. This was the closest to Australia that I had been since my arrival in Ireland and I was feeling a little misty-eyed. All hands were called to the junior ratings mess for a briefing on Singapore. At the end, the Captain said he had a little presentation to make – somehow he had gotten wind of the fact that the next day was my 21st birthday! I was given some ornamental rope work from the bosun, who is an expert in the field. I must admit I was pleasantly surprised and a little red-faced after the clapping died down but that was nothing compared to what was to happen the following day!

"It started off like any other day, with everyone busy getting the ship alongside and then getting her dressed with lights, flags and awnings, as well as preparing for functions. The temperature was fairly high, so we were all pretty hot, tired and dying to get off the ship for a chance to stretch our legs. We had been alongside about two hours when a delivery of flowers came to the ship from my mother for my birthday – that really made my day.

"When all was finished, we went into town to sample the excellent shopping of Orchard Road. Then it was back to the ship, to get ready for a reception at the Irish Ambassador's residence that we were all invited to. Drinks were served and soon after, a buffet-style dinner was on the way with an array of fresh fruit for dessert. As the evening drew in, and the sun disappeared, I heard shouts of 'Happy Birthday' coming towards me. The Irish Ambassador himself presented me with my 21st birthday cake and gave me my 21st birthday kiss! I was so surprised that I was actually speechless and could only stand there smiling, and stammering 'Thank You', as I shook hands with everyone. It was definitely one of the best birthday surprises I have ever had. Much as I miss my colleagues on LE EMER, I have memories of my 21st birthday that I will always cherish. Thank you, Ambassador Lyons."

SINGAPORE

**Lt Commander
Gerard O'Flynn,
Captain LE NIAMH**

Lt Commander O'Flynn welcomes
Irish Ambassador HE Brendan Lyons
on board LE NIAMH. Also in picture
are Commander Mark Mellett and
Commanding Officer RSS JUSTICE
(host ship), Major Ang Yong Lee, and
Navigating Officer RSS JUSTICE, Lt Eng
Han Chuen Adrian, liaison officer to
LE NIAMH while she was in Singapore

NIAMH arrived in Singapore ahead of schedule on Wednesday, 6 March, and anchored in the Straits of Singapore in an area known as the Man Of War anchorage.

In approaching Singapore, one is immediately struck by a skyline of skyscrapers, architecturally pleasing, intermixed with rich green plantations. From the ship's anchorage that night, the crew had a perfect view of the beautifully-lit buildings, all conveying an impression of a city buzzing with life.

Approaching Singapore from the north, the passage is through the Straits of Malacca, one of the busiest maritime areas in the world where sophisticated traffic management procedures are in place, all requiring a high degree of professionalism and concentration on the part of ship's officers. Large numbers of small fishing vessels, often difficult to see, add to the navigational challenges in the area.

On Thursday, 7 March, NIAMH berthed at the World Trade Centre, one of the most prestigious berths in Singapore, which was secured thanks to the efforts of Irish Ambassador, HE Brendan Lyons. The berth provided an ideal location for hosting functions, combining secure access and privacy with wonderful scenery.

Sentosa Island, located just half a kilometre to the south, provided a wonderful backdrop, with many of its world-class tourist attractions clearly visible from the reception area. In 2000, the island's attracted almost four million visitors - testifimony to its success.

On arrival, the ship was met by the Irish Ambassador, HE Brendan Lyons, Enterprise Ireland representatives Michael Garvey and KB Lim, Port officials, and Major Ang Yong Lee, Commanding Officer of RSS JUSTICE, the Republic of Singapore Navy host ship and liaison to the Singapore Navy for the visit. The navigating officer of the RSS JUSTICE, Lt Eng Han Chuen Adrian, was the ship's Liaison Officer. He was a most amiable host, attending to all of the ship's needs with courtesy and efficiency.

The ship's company immediately set about preparing NIAMH for the hectic four-day entertainment schedule that lay ahead. Receptions were to be held on the ship's Flag deck, and preparations included the erection of lights, flags and three sets of awnings, provisioning of bars and food serving areas, and organisation of equipment, etc.

As with all such visits, protocol demanded that the ship's Captain pay formal calls on local dignitaries. Calls were made on the Lord Mayor, senior Navy and Army

51

ABOVE LEFT, Singapore Navy Officers visiting LE NIAMH, with Lt Han Chuen Adrian, RSS liaison officer to NIAMH on the left and Lt Commander Gerard O'Flynn on the right ABOVE RIGHT, Lt Commander O'Flynn with Col Kevin Santa Maria, Commander of Coastal Command of the Singapore Navy

officers, the Chairman of the Port Authority and others. NIAMH's captain Lt Commander Gerard O'Flynn's military call of protocol was to the Commander of Coastal Command of the Singapore Navy. Lt Commander O'Flynn was pleasantly surprised when he discovered that the current holder of that appointment was Col Kevin Santa Maria, a fellow student, and good friend, from a year-long UK Royal Navy naval operations course back in 1988. Small world!

Later on Thursday, the Irish Ambassador and the Captain jointly hosted lunch onboard NIAMH. Guests included: Rear Admiral Lui Tuck Yew, Chief of the Singapore Navy; Col Tan Kai Hoe, Deputy Fleet Commander, Singapore Navy; Col Kevin Santa Maria, Coastal Commander; Vincent Lin, Port of Singapore Authority; and Captain Khon Shen Ping, Maritime Port Authority, Singapore.

That afternoon, a group of Australian and New Zealand naval officers visited the ship, accompanied by David McMillan, vice president of Kvaerner Masa Marine and Roger Coleman, MD of Babcock Defence Systems Australia. The group were viewing the ship as part of current procurement programmes in the two countries for ships similar to the "ROISIN" class. (LE ROISIN is NIAMH's sister-ship and gives the class its name.)

Later that evening, Ambassador Lyons kindly hosted the ship's company to a barbecue at the Ambassador's Residence. For one member of the ship's company, the evening will always hold a special memory – Telegraphist Victoria Kelly was celebrating her 21st birthday that day, and was presented with a birthday cake by Ambassador Lyons at the barbecue, with no shortage of offers of 21st birthday kisses from her colleagues.

Over 20 members of the ship's company had an early start on Friday morning, as they proceeded on a tour of Singaporean Naval training facilities, including a state-of-

ABOVE, Networking in action at functions on board LE NIAMH

the-art simulators. This equipment is of particular interest for Navy personnel, in the light of plans to develop a National Maritime College on Department of Defence-owned lands in Ringaskiddy, Cork, as a joint venture between the Cork Institute of Technology and the Navy.

On Friday morning also, IONA Technologies, one of 22 Irish companies with a permanent presence in Singapore, availed of NIAMH's facilities to host a press and client reception onboard. The IONA party included Patrick O'Brien, vice president of product strategy, and Michael Veretto, vice president Asia-Pacific.

Ireland's main exports to Singapore include telecommunications & IT software, engineering processing and services, food and food preparation, financial services and commodities. Along with Malaysia, Singapore is one of Ireland's main markets in the region. All of the Irish companies in Singapore were represented at a reception held onboard later that evening, for Irish

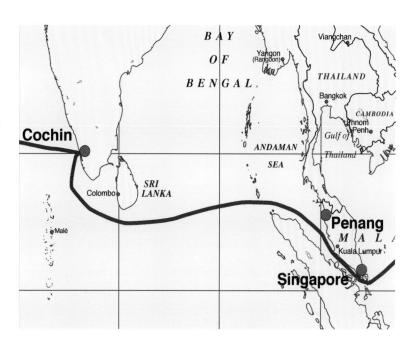

Republic of Singapore

- Population: 4,131,200 (July 2001)
- Capital: Singapore
- Port Visited by NIAMH: Singapore
- Irish Ambassador: HE Hugh Swift (HE Brendan Lyons was Ambassador at time of NIAMH's visit)
- Enterprise Ireland representative: KB Lim
- Enterprise Ireland clients active in Singapore include:
Amagruss Sensors Ltd, Atlanco Ltd, Baltimore Technologies, CCM Software Services Ltd, CR2 Ltd, Eontec, Icon PLC, Interactive Enterprise, Kerry Ingredients (Ireland) Ltd, Kingspan Ltd, O'Brien's Irish Sandwich Bars, PPI Adhesives Ltd, Project Management Ltd, Proscon Systems Ltd, Scientific Systems Ltd, SmartForce Ireland Ltd, Spectel Ltd, Waterford Wedgwood PLC, Xiam Ltd.

Visit – Key Facts:
- Number of functions: 7
- Number of visiting decision-makers: 191
- Total number of visitors: 680

companies and key buyers. The event was jointly hosted by Ambassador Lyons and NIAMH's Captain, with over 200 guests attending. Enterprise Ireland representatives included Singapore director, KB Lim, Michael Garvey, Enterprise Ireland's chief in Asia, and Anthony Courtney, Enterprise Ireland's representative in Malaysia at that time. Ambassador Lyons noted that the NIAMH's visit provided an excellent location for Enterprise Ireland and the Embassy to host on "home ground" Ireland's existing and potential customers in Singapore. The publicity generated by the visit, and the use that Irish companies made of it, strengthened Singapore's awareness of a modern Ireland as a quality source of technology and expertise.

Before departing the ship, guests were presented with a gift pack that included a bottle of Bailey's Irish Cream (an extremely popular drink locally), a Philip Gray print of LE NIAMH, as well as brochures and promotional literature.

On Saturday morning, a visiting group of Singaporean Navy personnel from host ship RSS JUSTICE were given a guided tour of NIAMH. DATAC Controls also hosted a presentation and technical demonstrations onboard.

On Saturday afternoon, Ambassador Lyons formally launched "Irish Week" at a reception onboard for over 400 guests. The reception coincided with an Open Day for Irish families, and all the children (and some adults) were presented with gift packs, including ship's baseball caps and merchandise sponsored by Kerrygold and its Singapore distributor, Lam Soon Pte. Ltd, which is active on behalf of the Irish Dairy Board in selling Irish butter and cheese throughout the region. The Irish community were raising funds to support the Singaporean Special Olympics team,

who will be based in Arklow, County Wicklow, for the summer games, which will be held in Ireland in 2003. A local Irish band, ironically named "Gan Ainm" (Irish for "Without a Name"), provided live music at the two main receptions.

Meanwhile, back onboard, the ship had to be prepared for sea, and all equipment secured and stored away, for an 0600 Monday morning start, and departure from Singapore before 0700. There were plenty of ships waiting to use NIAMH's valued berth.

Thus the first major stopover in the Asian deployment ended. A hectic weekend for everyone and still the crew managed to get to see the city as well.

L/S Frank Goss and A/S Siobhan Fennell entertain guests

Singapore consists of the main island of Singapore and some 63 other islands. Situated approximately 137 kilometres north of the Equator, Singapore is a prosperous city-state that has overcome its lack of natural resources to become one of the powerhouse economies of Asia. It has an average daily temperature of 27 degrees, all year round. In terms of sunshine hours, it has a year-round daily average of almost 12 hours (Ireland has only 3.7 hours). Singapore has a population of four million, yet its total land area is roughly the same as County Louth, in Ireland.

In less than 200 years since its founding by Sir Stafford Raffles, Singapore has transformed itself from a swampy island to a modern industrial nation. Over the years, it has been controlled by Malaysia, Britain and Japan. However, in 1965, it became a fully sovereign state and a republic.

Modern Singapore is a city of concrete, glass, freeways and shopping centers, providing the visitor with a fascinating choice of activities ranging from restaurants to cater for every conceivable palate, western-style clothes, and arrays of electronic goods. It even has its quota of Irish pubs including Muddy Murphys, Fr Flanagans and Shamus O'Donnells, where manager Pat Grennan made NIAMH's crew all feel very much at home.

Singapore is one of the most cosmopolitan countries in Asia. It is a secular state with a multiracial and multicultural mix: every ethnic community is entitled to practice its own religion and way of life. This unifying policy has resulted in a rich cultural heritage.

The Republic of Singapore Navy is headed by the Chief of Navy, and divided into four Commands. The Coastal Command is equipped with Patrol Vessels and Mine Counter-Measure Vessels. A separate Command controls missile corvettes, missile gunboats, and multi-role vessels known as LSTs (Landing Ships Tanks), whose tasks include humanitarian aid. This Command also operates the fleet of four submarines. The other two Commands control training and logistics.

Singapore is the world's busiest port in terms of shipping tonnage. At any one time, there are more than 800 ships in port. Singapore is also the world's top bunkering (ship refuelling) port, as well as one of the world's largest oil refining centres. The combined refining capacity is over one million barrels per day.

Singapore is the world's largest exporting nation on a *per capita* basis. It is Ireland's 11th largest trading partner, and 6th largest import supplier.

HONG KONG

0400 hrs on 15 March, 2002 and NIAMH is in position Latitude 21° 57'. 5 N 114° 18'. 6 E, approximately 16 nautical miles south of the approaches to Hong Kong harbour. Sea conditions are excellent, visibility is good and the volume of local fishing and commercial traffic is enormous. The Officer of the Watch passes a helm order to the seaman on the wheel, and instantly the ship responds and passes clear of the next fishing boat, and continues to navigate her way towards the famous and historic port of Hong Kong. NIAMH continues to weave through the surface traffic and, as the first shards of the dawn begin to break, she arrives at the designated position to embark a harbour pilot. The pilot assists the ship's Captain in bringing the ship through the narrow seaways between Hong Kong Island and the New Territories, before mooring to a buoy in Victoria Harbour.

As soon as NIAMH had secured to the buoy, a floating pontoon was placed alongside to facilitate the embarkation of visitors and guests. The first person to board the ship was the Flag Officer, Commodore John Kavanagh, with the Minister of Defense, Michael Smith TD and his official party, together with the Chief of Staff (COS) of the Defence Forces, Lt General Colm Mangan, HE Ambassador Declan Connolly from the Beijing Embassy, Peter Coyle, Enterprise Ireland's Executive Director for Asia, and David O'Callaghan, Secretary General of the Department of Defence, all of whom had arrived in Hong Kong the previous day. Dr Chok-Hung Lee, Ireland's Honorary Consul in Hong Kong, was also present and played a large part in ensuring the official schedule went smoothly.

Lt Commander O'Flynn also welcomed aboard a film crew from RTE, Ireland's national broadcasting service, headed by presenter Derek Davis, who timed their visit to Hong Kong to coincide with the NIAMH to film some segments for his programme "Out of the Blue". After filming around Hong Kong, it was decided that the RTE crew would sail with the ship as far as Shanghai to shoot other segments for the programme.

As daylight dawned, Hong Kong's fantastic skyline was revealed all around. To the south lay the towering skyscrapers of Hong Kong. Closest to NIAMH was the immense Hong Kong Convention & Exhibition Centre, built at the time of the hand-over of the former colony to the People's Republic of China. Straddled along the

OPPOSITE PAGE, Courtesy call on Major General Wang Xiaojun, Deputy Forces Commander, People's Liberation Army
ABOVE, Hong Kong from Victoria Peak

S/Lt Eric Timon, Gunnery Officer

ABOVE LEFT, Flag Officer Commodore John Kavanagh presents David O'Callaghan. Secretary-General, Irish Department of Defence with a Philip Gray painting of NIAMH
ABOVE RIGHT, Commander Mark Mellett, Chief of Staff Lt General Colm Mangan, Flag Officer Commodore John Kavanagh and Lt Commander Gerard O'Flynn, Captain LE NIAMH

waterfront were the Civic Tower, Bank of America Tower, and the Bank of China Tower to name but a few. The entire city of Hong Kong appeared to be sandwiched between the sea, and the peaks of Aberdeen and Pok Fu Lam Country Parks, to their summit of 552 metres at Victoria Peak. To the North, Kowloon was ringed by the mountainous Galden Hill and Lion Rock Country Parks rising to an even more impressive height of 602 metres at Kowloon Peak. It was a fantastic view, which all visitors to the ship would enjoy.

Mindful of NIAMH's role as a platform for the trade mission, the ship's company set about preparing the ship for the busy schedule of corporate events planned for the duration of the stay.

The profile of the Calls of Protocol was raised due to the presence onboard of the Flag Officer, Commodore John Kavanagh. Calls were made on Timothy Tong, Acting Secretary for Security, and on Major General Wang Xiaojun, Deputy Force Commander of the People's Liberation Army.

Meanwhile, David and Noel from Delaney's and Dublin Jack Irish bars had come onboard to brief the crew on the 'dos and don'ts' of Hong Kong, etc.

That evening, the Minister for Defence hosted a dinner onboard for approximately 40 people. He made a personal presentation to the ship of a piece of Tipperary Crystal, representing his home county in Ireland. The Chief of Staff also made a presentation to the ship's Captain – the first occasion on which a Chief of Staff made such a presentation to an Irish ship on service abroad.

On Saturday, 16 March, the Flag Officer, Captain, officers and senior NCOs from NIAMH attended the St Patrick's Day Ball as guests of Enterprise Ireland in the Grand Hyatt Hotel, where the Minister was the Guest of Honour. Organised by the Irish community, the event is regarded as the social event of the year in Hong Kong. Although the St Patrick's Society, chaired by Tom Mulvey this year, has organised the annual Ball for 65 years, this

ABOVE LEFT, Lt Commander Gerard O'Flynn, Captain LE NIAMH, Minister for Defence Michael Smith TD and Peter Coyle, Executive Director – Asia, Enterprise Ireland
ABOVE RIGHT, Fr Des Campion, Roman Catholic Chaplain to the Forces celebrating St Patrick's Day Mass on board LE NIAMH, assisted by Cadets Dominic Kelly and Elaine Browne

was the first time that the event was graced by the Irish Defence Forces in full military dress.

On St Patrick's Day itself, a special parade and shamrock blessing ceremony was held onboard NIAMH, and was attended by a representative group of the Irish community. The ceremony began with the arrival of the Minister, Chief of Staff and the Flag Officer on the Flag Deck. The Navy's Roman Catholic Chaplain, Fr Des Campion, blessed the shamrock, which was then presented to the ship's company by the Minister, Chief of Staff, Flag Officer and ship's Captain. Following the celebration of a Roman Catholic Mass, Irish stew was served, washed down with an occasional pint of Guinness or glass of Bailey's. The celebrations were recorded for subsequent transmission by RTE for the St Patrick's Day roundup on the main evening television news back home in Ireland.

It was a nostalgic day for members of the Irish community present, as they stood on a 78-metre by 14-metre piece of Ireland (a naval vessel is the sovereign territory of the country of origin). All around them were NIAMH's crew, speaking with welcoming accents from the length and breadth of the country. There were many examples present of Irish people who had married and settled in Hong Kong, for whom it was the first time any of their families had set foot on "Irish territory".

The officers and crew of the NIAMH hosted numerous Irish families and their children on tours of the ship during the day and, in the evening, the Ministerial party and senior officers were guests of the Royal College of Surgeons in Ireland at their worldwide Alumni Dinner at the Aberdeen Marina Club.

Over the course of the next few days, NIAMH hosted a range of corporate lunches, presentations and cocktail parties for a number of Irish companies and agencies. The Irish Business Forum, which acts as the Irish Chamber of Commerce in Hong Kong, currently chaired by Mervyn Jacob, had a major reception on board. Sixteen Irish companies have located regional offices in Hong Kong,

ABOVE LEFT AND RIGHT, visitors to
LE NIAMH on St Patrick's Day

selling into the Greater China market. Many more Irish people work in Hong Hong for multinational companies and for the local Government, so the Irish business scene is quite well represented in Hong Kong.

Bord Bia (the Irish Food Board) and Bord Iascaigh Mhara (the Irish Fisheries Board) took the opportunity to expose local companies to Irish food and fish respectively at two lunches catered on board during the week. Minister of State for Food, Noel Davern TD was guest of honour for these events, which coincided with his return trip to Ireland from a promotional programme in Australia.

In addition to organising these business events, Enterprise Ireland also held a reception for its key contacts in Hong Kong and Ambassador Connolly used the opportunity to cultivate contacts in the local Government. Given that this was the only port where the ship was anchored off-shore, credit is due to Patrick Yau, manager of Enterprise Ireland's Hong Kong and South China office,

and to his assistant Ms W. Lee for their organisation of the events – and particularly in arranging the logistics, including the fleet of water-taxis to ferry guests to, and from, the pier.

Ashore, the crew of NIAMH participated in many sporting events. A team match was played against the Hong Kong Police Maritime Division. A 10-a-side Gaelic football game was played against a local Irish team. Three of the ship's crew, all Defence Force rugby players, Lt Owen Mullowney, A/Sea Fergus Blackmore and Leading Seaman Paul Shanahan, participated in the Hong Kong 10s rugby competition. On Saturday afternoon, the Hong Kong Gaelic Athletic Association (GAA) Club, headed by Ronan Delaney, invited the Navy side to a mixed GAA/Rugby "tournament" at which, despite valiant efforts, the NIAMH team succumbed to the very talented local team.

The Irish community in Hong Kong made the officers and crew of NIAMH very welcome. Hospitality was

ABOVE LEFT, visitors to the bridge guided by Cadet Stuart Donaldson
ABOVE RIGHT, Minister for Defence Michael Smith TD on camera

offered by many local people and organisations – special thanks is due to Noel Smyth and his people at the Delaney's Group of Restaurants and Pubs, and to Nigel Hughes and to Joe Oxley for their offers of facilities at the Hong Kong Yacht Club and the Kowloon Club respectively.

Prior to the departure for Shanghai on 21 March, a number of NIAMH's cadets left for Ireland, having completed their tour of duty, and were replaced by others, who flew in from Ireland. The Flag officer joined NIAMH for the Shanghai and Tokyo stages of the voyage and the RTE crew also joined the ship for the Shanghai stage.

Hong Kong on St Patrick's Day will always hold special memories for everybody who was onboard NIAMH that day, especially the strong Irish community, who are well organised and doing marvellous work in projecting a most positive image of Ireland.

Hong Kong Special Administrative Region, People's Republic of China

- Population:
  7,210,505 Hong Kong SAR
- Capital: Beijing
- Port Visited by NIAMH:
  Hong Kong
- Irish Ambassador (based in Beijing)
  HE Declan Connolly
- Irish Honorary Consul:
  HE Dr Chok-Hung Lee
- Enterprise Ireland Manager for
  China/Hong Kong: Alan Hobbs
- Enterprise Ireland representative in
  Hong Kong: Patrick Yau
- Enterprise Ireland clients active in
  Hong Kong include:
  Baltimore Technologies, DATAC
  Control International Ltd, Intuition
  Publishing Ltd, Iona Technologies PLC,
  Kingspan Ltd, Logica Aldiscon Ltd,
  Network365 Ltd, PARC Aviation Ltd,
  Parthus Ireland Ltd, Smurfit Ireland
  Ltd, Trintech (Holdings) Ltd, Waterford
  Wedgwood PLC.

Visit – Key Facts:
- Number of functions: 11
- Number of visiting decision-makers:
  300
- Total number of visitors: 769

Hong Kong was originally a neglected part of the Qing dynasty empire inhabited by farmers, fishermen and pirates. The territory formally became a British possession on 26 June 1843 so that Britain could exercise more control in their trade of opium with the Chinese. A second Anglo-Chinese war in 1860 gave the British the Kowloon peninsula, and 40 years later they also claimed the New Territories. Instead of annexing this colony outright the British agreed to a 99-year lease and on 30 June 1997 as Governor Chris Patten struck the Union Jack for the last time, the Special Administrative Region of Hong Kong was born. This transition period will last until 2047 when Hong Kong will become fully integrated with the Peoples Republic of China.

Hong Kong still remains a centre of capitalism. Free enterprise, free trade, very low taxes, excellent infrastructure and a hard working labour force are key strengths of the Hong Kong economy. Service industries employ more than 75 % of Hong Kong's workforce, and account for nearly 80 % of its GDP.

AN IRISH HONG KONG RESIDENT'S VIEW

To Hong Kong natives, long-term foreign residents, and visitors alike, Victoria Harbour is one of the most spectacular settings in the world. And there, on 15 March 2002, before our eyes, just off Causeway Bay, was a piece of Irish territory afloat in the "Fragrant Harbour" (a literal translation of Hong Kong). During the week that followed, the LE Niamh became an integral part of life for many of us, and there were few who did not have the pleasure of being onboard or meeting her officers and crew around Hong Kong.

The Irish community here enjoys much *ceol, craic agus caint* in March every year, but the St Patrick's festival in 2002 was on a different scale, due entirely to the presence of our unique Irish visitor. The Irish have been in Hong Kong since the earliest days of the territory's history as a Crown Colony. The first recorded mention of a celebration of St Patrick's Day in Hong Kong was in 1847, and there have been few years since then when March 17th has not been marked with appropriate festivities. For the past 65 or so years, the St Patrick's Society of Hong Kong has organised an annual ball, although this is by no means the only means of marking St Patrick's Day, and as many or more revellers are to be found in the Irish pubs that have sprung up in Hong Kong during the past decade.

This year's Annual Ball was held at the Grand Hyatt on March 16th, providing the first opportunity for the NIAMH team to meet the Irish community here. We had the honour of the company of not only the Minister for Defence, Michael Smith TD, but also the massed senior ranks of the Irish defence establishment, along with Lt Commander Gerard O'Flynn and some of his officers. The night is always a glamorous one, but there is no doubt that the many military dress uniforms on show that night added a level of style that we're unlikely to see again.

On the following morning, many bleary-eyed partygoers were welcomed aboard the NIAMH by Lt Commander O'Flynn to celebrate Mass, an event that was recorded by RTE, leading to many of our number getting calls from home to say that they'd been spotted on the evening news. The afternoon saw the crew welcome many of our children aboard. Always happy to be on the water, they were enthralled by the NIAMH, and captivated by the warm welcome of the crew members who showed them around. Their parents were in most cases captivated more by the opportunity to drink Dublin-brewed Guinness on Irish "soil" in the middle of Hong Kong!

Through the days that followed, Captain and crew welcomed large numbers of the Irish community and our friends aboard, and provided us with unique hospitality, and the fondest of memories. The crew of the NIAMh also got to see some of us on dry land, and more than a few found their way to Delaney's in Wanchai, the unofficial capital of Irish Hong Kong. Wherever we met the crew, we were invariably delighted by their company, and proud of the job that they were doing as ambassadors for Ireland.

Harry O'Neill
Irish Business Forum, Hong Kong

SHANGHAI, CHINA

**Lt Commander Gerard O'Flynn,
Captain LE NIAMH**

When the People's Liberation Army (PLA) Navy ship HUAINAN bade farewell to LE NIAMH at the entrance to Shanghai harbour, it marked the end of an historic Irish naval visit to China. The 12-day visit, incorporating a week in Hong Kong, and five days in Shanghai, marked the first occasion on which an Irish Navy ship had visited the People's Republic of China.

From a mariner's perspective, Shanghai must be regarded as one of the most challenging navigation passages anywhere in the world. Although both Singapore and Hong Kong handle larger volumes of trade, the sheer density of traffic, ranging from large container ships to coasters, barges and a host of other craft, ranks Shanghai as one of the busiest ports in the world.

The passage up river to Shanghai is approximately 68 miles long, commencing in the buoyed channel at 31° 06N 122° 30E, in an area known as Changjiang Kou. Tidal streams of up to five knots were experienced in the approaches, some of which were flowing at right angles to the channel. Given the length of the approach, overtaking in the waterway is frequent, and practised by vessels of all sizes – up to six vessels abeam, some travelling in opposite directions, were seen at times. Intensive fishing is also a feature of these pilotage waters, and crossing traffic is a regularly encountered hazard. The scale of activity is

perhaps best appreciated by comparing the area with rush hour traffic in a busy urban area.

NIAMH arrived at Shanghai approaches on Monday, 25 March at 0600, and rendezvoused with the PLA Navy frigate HUAINAN. NIAMH proceeded in company with the frigate, overtaking several large merchant ships in the process. Course and speed adjustments were frequent, to deal with situations varying from crossing traffic, to narrower areas of the channel, in addition to large volumes of traffic departing Shanghai.

About 49 miles into the estuary, in an area known as Huangpu Jiang, NIAMH rendezvoused with a PLA Navy patrol boat. The PLA Navy Liaison Officer, pilot and several officials, including immigration and quarantine personnel were transferred to the Irish ship. The officials met with the ship's Executive Officer, Lt Owen Mullowney, and the administrative details of the port entry were dealt with, including general certification, garbage disposal, onboard environmental policy, and placing of orders for replenishment of supplies and foodstuffs.

The passage to Shanghai continued, and it soon became apparent that, for ceremonial reasons, NIAMH was expected to pass a series of points at pre-determined times, thus calling for more detailed navigation planning and execution. The passage to Shanghai begins in earnest at a

ABOVE LEFT, Flag Officer Commodore
John Kavanagh, with Lt Commander
O'Flynn in left background, being greeted
on arrival at Shanghai by Rear Admiral Gu
Wen Gen, Deputy Commander of East
China Sea Fleet, PLA Navy
ABOVE RIGHT, Bosun PO Niall Dunne
guiding visitors onboard LE NIAMH

point where the Huangpu River flows into the Yangtse River. The PLA Navy escort frigate departed, but two PLA Navy river patrol boats continued to follow, and the lead was taken by four Harbour Police escort vessels. The channel became much narrower than the outer estuary, but had a higher volume of traffic, including large container ships, bulk carriers, coasters, barges and other craft. The passage from the mouth of the Huangpu River to the berth involves a distance of 19 miles. NIAMH was generally in an overtaking situation, and had the advantage of being categorised as priority traffic, with its route being cleared by the escort vessels travelling ahead with flashing police lights and sirens. Despite this support, manoeuvring space was tight, and high levels of concentration were called for.

NIAMH berthed at the Yangtse River Wharf after an eight-hour passage through an intensely busy waterway. Ordinarily, the bridge team would relax after such a passage, but it was straight into a ceremonial programme.

The ship's arrival was marked by the presence of a PLA Navy Band. On stepping off the gangway, Flag Officer Commodore John Kavanagh and NIAMH's Captain were greeted by Rear Admiral Gu Wen Gen, Deputy Commander of the East China Sea Fleet, Captain Xu Ji Wen, Commander of the Shanghai Naval Base, Mr Yuan Gongxia, Deputy Director of SFAO, in the presence of the Irish Ambassador, HE Declan Connolly, the Irish Consul General, Geoffrey Keating, Michael Garvey of Enterprise Ireland and Ms Renee Wu, manager of Enterprise Ireland's Shanghai Office. The arrival ceremony consisted of a short exchange of greetings, aided by an interpreter, and presentation of bouquets of flowers to the Flag Officer and NIAMH's Captain. The ceremony received widespread media coverage on both press and TV, including coverage on main news bulletins, and the publication of a photograph in the *China Daily News* newspaper.

On completion of the arrival ceremony, the Flag

Officer and Captain proceeded on a series of formal calls of protocol, which included calls on Vice Mayor Feng Guoqin in Government Buildings in People's Square, and Vice Admiral Wang Yucheng, Chief of Staff of PLA Navy at the Wusong Naval Base. On arrival at the Naval Base, Commodore Kavanagh inspected a Guard of Honour, formed in his honour.

NIAMH's calls of protocol in China followed a standard format. They were held in large ornate reception halls. All guests were seated, in a rectangular format, with the hosts and the principal guests at the head of the seating area. The host made a short welcoming address which was translated, then the principal guest replied. There followed a conversation between host and guests, which, because of the need for interpretation, for all practical purposes could be regarded as a series of short speeches. The ceremonies, which usually lasted about 20 minutes, concluded with an exchange of gifts. Following the Calls of Protocol, the Flag

FAR LEFT, Chinese sailor with a special envelope to commemorate LE NIAMH's historic visit.
LEFT, A/S Sharon Darbysigns a commemorative envelope for visitors

ABOVE LEFT, visitors on board LE NIAMH
ABOVE RIGHT, PLA Navy Officer and two
irish guests onboard LE NIAMH

Officer and NIAMH's Captain joined a representative group from the ship on a guided tour of the PL A Navy frigate HUAINAN. A party of 25 from NIAMH later attended a banquet hosted by the PLA Navy Chief of Staff in honour of the visit.

In association with Enterprise Ireland, NIAMH hosted a series of events aimed at promoting Ireland and Irish business in China. The ship was berthed in a highly visible part of Shanghai, close to the Bund area, an internationally famous old colonial area of Shanghai, featuring beautifully-preserved old buildings. Directly opposite lay Pudong, an area of Shanghai that has been extensively developed in recent years, with buildings such as the Jingmao Tower, which houses the Hyatt Hotel in its upper levels, making it the highest hotel in the world, and the Oriental Pearl TV Tower, a futuristic design incorporating two large spheres on supporting legs. All of the buildings when lit at night made a spectacular backdrop for various receptions, held on the ship's Flag-deck.

On Tuesday, following a lunch onboard earlier in the day attended by local dignitaries, a diplomatic reception co-hosted by Ambassador Declan Connolly was attended by 175 members of the local business community.

Many other business-orientated functions were held during the week. Bord Iascaigh Mhara, the body tasked with developing Ireland's sea-fishing and aquaculture industries, held a briefing and corporate lunch for 40 clients and contacts. MEI-RELSA, which co-ordinates the teaching of English to international students in Ireland, and IONA Technology held separate client briefings onboard. Enterprise Ireland held a reception for the Information Technology sector, which was attended by 150 guests. MEI-RELSA also held an evening reception for over 100 guests. Weather was comparable to Ireland, with outbreaks of rain. The use of patio-style gas heaters —organised by Peter Mulcahy of O'Malley's pub – ensured that nobody

got too cold. The excellent fine canapés supplied by Brendan Brophy of the Dublin Exchange added to the ambience and Irish party atmosphere.

Provision of ship's services was co-ordinated by the PLA Navy, and a reception in their honour was hosted onboard on the eve of NIAMH's departure. Members of the PLA Navy were also given guided tours of the ship.

The ship was open to the public for a four-hour period on Thursday afternoon, and attracted a constant flow of people. The attendance was estimated at well over 2,000, and Chinese officials indicated that several more thousands had sought tickets for the visit.

To mark the first visit by an Irish Navy ship to Shanghai, a special commemorative envelope was issued, featuring a picture of the ship digitally superimposed on the water-front of Shanghai. Several thousands of these were sold, hundreds of which were personally signed by Commodore Kavanagh and the Captain. The task of

Shanghai, People's Republic of China

- Population: 1,273,111,290 (July 2001) China, 13,053,700 (Shanghai)
- Capital: Beijing
- Port Visited by NIAMH: Shanghai
- Irish Ambassador – China: HE Declan Connolly
- Irish Consul-General – Shanghai: Geoffrey Keating
- Enterprise Ireland Manager for China: Alan Hobbs
- Enterprise Ireland representative in Shanghai: Renee Wu
- Enterprise Ireland clients active in China include: Baltimore Technologies, Bord Iascaigh Mhara (the Irish Fisheries Board), Clearstream Technologies Ltd, Eurologic Systems Ltd, Glen Dimplex Exports Ltd, Infocell Ltd, Iona Technologies PLC, Network365 Ltd, Openet Telecom Ltd, Shannon Engine Support Ltd, Sigma Wireless Technologies Ltd, SmartForce Ireland Ltd, Smurfit Ireland Ltd, Trinity Biotech Manufacturing Ltd, Unilokomotive Ltd, Waterford Wedgwood PLC and several of the major Irish universities.

Visit – Key Facts:
- Number of functions: 11
- Number of visiting decision-makers: 209
- Total number of visitors: 2412

signing the envelopes was referred to as "homework" by the PLA Navy Liaison Officer. In fact, nearly every member of the crew obliged the autograph-hunters by signing and stamping many thousands of first day issues with the ship's stamp.

Other visitors to the ship included members of the Irish community and a group fundraising for the Irish Wheelchair association. This busy programme left little time for sightseeing, but most crew members had at least one full day off. Two sporting fixtures were fitted in, including a Gaelic football game against Shanghai GAA club, played in the rugby grounds of Pudong and a soccer game against the PLA Navy. Shanghai has three Irish pubs – The Dublin Exchange, O'Malleys and the Blarney Stone – all of which went to great lengths to support the visit, including the organising of bus tours of the area.

NIAMH's visit to Shanghai formed an important element of the Government's Asia-Pacific Strategy, which is focused on the foreign earnings potential of the Asian markets. One of the key challenges is to increase awareness of Ireland in countries where economic and political links have traditionally been weak, and where the name "Ireland" meets with limited public recognition. To this end, it is to be hoped that that the presence of NIAMH in China has contributed to this important national objective.

Onboard NIAMH, the outstanding memory will be the navigation challenge of entering and departing Shanghai harbour, accurately described as "a Formula One Grand Prix in slow motion".

The warm and friendly welcome provided by the PLA Navy will also be a cherished memory. Their support and friendship was greatly appreciated.

On Thursday, 28 April, Commodore Kavanagh, accompanied by Commander Mark Mellett and Lt Owen Mullowney, travelled to Beijing at the invitation of Admiral Shi, Commander in Chief of the PLA Navy. The Admiral hosted a dinner in their honour, with HE Irish Ambassador Declan Connolly also in attendance. The Irish Navy officers later visited the Great Wall of China and the Forbidden City. The picture right shows Commodore Kavanagh with Admiral Shi.

Traditional waterside temple, Shanghai

China, or to give it its full title, The People's Republic of China, is one of the largest countries in the world. It is approximately the size of Europe and has a population of 1.25 billion. It has a young population with almost 24% under the age of 15.

China's economic policy is changing dramatically, and wide-scale privatisation is taking place. Its wealth is concentrated in large urban areas, in cities such as Shanghai. This new economic policy, known as the "open door" policy, aims to decentralise the economic system, and to attract overseas investment into China.

China is the third largest country in the world, and has the world's seventh largest economy. China has experienced 20 years of unprecedented economic growth, during which the economy grew faster than any other economy in history, and incomes more than quadrupled. It is simultaneously changing from a rural to an urban society, and from a command economy to a market economy. Annual inflation rates have remained below 1.5% over the last few years, and GDP has grown at an annual rate of over 7%. Ireland has a negative trade balance with China, but the value of exports to China has increased considerably over recent years. In 1999, Irish exports to China were worth $125 million, an increase of 57% on the previous year, and 77% on the year before. In 2000, China was Ireland's 20th largest trading partner, 38th largest export market, and 13th largest source of imports. It is a priority market for certain sectors of Irish industry, especially high-tech products and chemicals.

Shanghai itself has a population of over 12 million, and is one of the most important cities in China. Many of China's most prominent politicians hail from Shanghai, including the President of China, Jiang Zemin and the Premier, Zhu Rong Ji, at the time of NIAMH's visit – the latter visited Ireland in 2001.

INCHEON, KOREA

LE NIAMH arrived in Incheon, Korea on April Fool's Day, Monday, 1 April 2002. On the morning of NIAMH's arrival, visibility was extremely poor and the port was closed to commercial traffic. NIAMH rendezvoused with the Republic of Korea Navy (ROKN) host ship DAECHON off Incheon at 0500 (local time), and proceeded in company towards the berth at the Naval Base. At over 9 metres, the tidal range in the port is one of the most extreme in the world. The ship was berthed on a floating pontoon within the Naval Base and, on berthing, the visibility was less than half of one ship's length – thus the ship was virtually alongside before the berth was actually visible, a source of much nervousness and tension on NIAMH's bridge. Ironically, long before any part of Korea was visible, a Naval band could be heard practising the Irish National Anthem, for the subsequent arrival ceremony. A rather memorable, if unusual, arrival into port.

The ship's arrival was marked by a greeting ceremony, incorporating a parade of the ship's companies of NIAMH and ROKN host ship DAECHON, a welcoming address by Admiral Lee of ROKN, Commander of Incheon Naval Sector Defence Command, a reply by the Flag Officer Commodore Kavanagh, and a presentation of flowers to the Flag Officer and NIAMH's Captain, in the presence of Irish Ambassador to Korea, HE Paul Murray.

Later that day, the Flag Officer and NIAMH's Captain, accompanied by Ambassador Murray, paid formal calls on Admiral Lee, on the Director General of Incheon Regional Maritime Affairs, and on the Mayor of Incheon.

At a time when Ireland seeks to enhance its profile in Asia, it is fortunate that much positive work has already been done by generations of Irish Religious Orders who have dedicated their missionary lives to education, medical care, and attending to the needs of the less well-off groups of society. The Irish Columban Fathers and Sisters have had

Lt Commander Gerard O'Flynn, Captain LE NIAMH

OPPOSITE PAGE: Lt Owen Mullowney and PO Joe Morrison with ROKN SEALS on NIAMH
BELOW: Lt Commander O'Flynn and Commodore John Kavanagh being welcomed to Incheon

ABOVE LEFT, Welcome ceremony, Incheon
ABOVE RIGHT, Sr Geraldine Ryan, Irish
Columban Sisters with Lt Commander
Michael Malone, Marine Engineering Officer
LE NIAMH

a long-term presence in Korea, and two Columban groups visited the ship. The ship hosted a group of 75 from the Kwangju mentally handicapped projects operated by Irish Columban Fathers. The group was given a tour of the ship and entertained to lunch onboard. A similar reception was provided for a group from the mentally handicapped project operated by the Columban Sisters.

Over the course of the three-day visit, thanks to the sterling work of Peter Ryan from the Irish Embassy and Ms Meejung Lee, who acts for Enterprise Ireland and IDA Ireland in Korea, lunches were hosted for naval and port authorities, government contacts, and a dinner for key business contacts. Two evening receptions, attended by over 350 diplomatic and business contacts were held onboard. MEI-RELSA, the coordinating and promoting body for the teaching of English in Ireland, held a very successful workshop, aimed at promoting Ireland as a suitable location in which to learn the English language.

The sporting highlight of the visit was a soccer match against an ROKN selection. A promising start saw the NIAMH team take an early and deserved two-goal lead but, following some astute Korean substitutions, the teams were level at half-time. In the second half, the Koreans added another goal to run out deserving winners, in a hard-fought and skillful match. Before the game, Admiral Lee of the ROKN was presented with an official Football Association of Ireland (FAI) World Cup tracksuit, which he promised to wear to Ireland's second round matches. NIAMH's team, of course, played all their matches in the official FAI World Cup strip, kindly presented by the FAI prior to departure from Ireland. After the game, several members of the ship's company visited Incheon's World Cup stadium.

The ROKN personnel were warm and pleasant hosts, and were generous with their time, sparing no effort to give everybody an opportunity to experience Korean life

ABOVE LEFT, reception onboard LE NIAMH with Lt Commander O'Flynn and Liaison Officer Lt Commander Jim Shalloo on left, Elizabeth Fitz-Simon, wife of Irish Ambassador HE Paul Murray, and Admiral Lee, ROKN, in centre and Lt Owen Mullowney, rear right
ABOVE RIGHT, Captain O'Flynn with Mr Yang Ho Cho, Honorary Consul-General of Ireland in Korea

and culture. The visit itself was hosted by Admiral Lee, whose enthusiasm was enhanced by Commodore John Kavanagh's rendition of the "Banks of my Own Lovely Lee"(the anthem of Cork, the Navy's home town) at one of the functions held in association with the visit.

Korea is a dynamic and progressive country, keen to establish itself as a focal point of trade in NE Asia. There can be little doubt that fostering closer links with Korea will be of critical importance to Ireland as it seeks to develop its Asian strategy.

It was also timely to have met with Ambassador Paul Murray, as he is the author of the seminal work on the writer, Lafcadio Hearn. Tokyo was to be NIAMH's next port of call and, for many years, the Japanese people knew of Ireland only as the homeland of this great Irish-Greek writer and interpreter of Japan. His achievements in Japan almost 100 years ago constitute the main historical links between the two countries.

Republic of Korea

- Population: 47,904,370 (July 2002)
- Capital: Seoul
- Port Visited by NIAMH: Incheon
- Irish Ambassador: HE Paul Murray
- Enterprise Ireland Manager for Korea: Declan Collins (based in Tokyo)
- Enterprise Ireland/IDA Ireland Representative in Seoul: Meejung Lee
- Enterprise Ireland clients active in Korea include:
  Betatherm Ireland Ltd, Bluebeam Ltd, Chanelle Veterinary Ltd, Cross Vetpharm Group Ltd, Davenham Engineering Ltd, Donegal Fish Products Ltd, Drive Right Holdings Ltd, Farran Technology Ltd, Iona Technologies PLC, Irish Distillers Ltd, Magee Weaving Ltd, Marigot Ltd, Multis Ltd, PARC Aviation Ltd, Parthus Ireland Ltd, Quest International Ireland Ltd, Scientific Systems Ltd, Sofrimar Ltd, UDV Operations Ireland Ltd, Univet Ltd.

Visit – Key Facts:
- Number of functions: 13
- Number of visiting decision-makers: 297
- Total number of visitors: 1030

Courtesy call to Admiral Lee, ROK Navy

Courtesy call to Mayor of Incheon

Visitors from Mokpo mentally handicapped projects operated by the Irish Columban Sisters

Visitors from Kwangju mentally handicapped projects operated by the Irish Columban Fathers

Captain O'Flynn and Commodor John Kavanagh with Dr Un-Nah Huh, National Assembly of Korea member

Commodore John Kavanagh and Irish Ambassador HE Paul Murray with Mr Oh-Yeon Na, Chairman of Korea Ireland Parlimentary Frendship Association and Mr Jae-Jin Shim of LG Electronics

INCHEON – BACKGROUND

Incheon is located in the central-western portion of the Korean peninsula, some 20 miles west of Seoul, and has a population of 2.6 million. It is entered from the Yellow Sea and, in addition to being an important naval base, is a busy and strategically-important commercial port. The city is seeking to establish itself as a major centre in north-east Asia, with a state-of-the-art international airport and seaport. It has traditionally identified itself as Korea's gateway to international trade. Its modern-day development can be traced to the Treaty of Commerce signed with the USA in 1882, and subsequent treaties agreed with other Western powers. Incheon prides itself on being the first Korean city to have had a train system, and later a telephone system. Historically, it is internationally recognised as the centre of gravity for General McArthur's Incheon landings, which proved to be a turning point of the Korean War of the 1950s. The DMZ (De-Militarised Zone), the border between North and South Korea, is approximately 25 miles from where NIAMH berthed.

Along with Japan, Korea was a co-host of the 2002 World Cup, and Incheon was a host city for first round matches between Costa Rica/Turkey, Denmark/France and Korea/Portugal. The stadium in Incheon, known as the Munhak stadium, named after the nearby Munhak mountain, is "all seated", with a capacity for 50,256 spectators. It is the centre-piece of a newly constructed sports complex, featuring a separate baseball stadium, swimming pool, and recreational areas. Connected by giant cables to 24 posts located around the stadium, the roof of the main stadium looks like the sail of a giant ship. Its use of a "cable membrane structure system" is designed to minimise the use of reinforced frames, or of support structures, within the spectator area. It is an incredibly impressive building, and very much symbolises the vibrancy, creativity, and skill that Korea wishes to portray to its world audience.

In 2001, Irish exports to Korea amounted to €700million, consisting mainly of electronic products, organic chemicals, and pharmaceuticals. Exports by Irish-owned companies are growing, particularly in the high-tech sectors. Seven Korean companies have direct operations in Ireland, including LG Electronics, which has a European R&D centre in Dublin, Korean Air, which has its European telemarketing office in Dublin, and Saehan Media, which manufactures videocassettes in Sligo. Other well-known Korean companies and brands trading in Ireland include Hyundai, Samsung, and Daewoo. To coincide with NIAMH's visit to Korea, a bilateral agreement was signed between the Irish and Korean Chambers of Commerce.

TOKYO, JAPAN

Looming out of the morning haze, the structure of Tokyo's famous Rainbow Bridge greeted NIAMH's arrival, towering over the ship as she slid through the waters of Tokyo Bay. As the Captain made his approach to Harumi Pier, the band of the Japanese Maritime Self Defence Force (JMSDF) struck up some jaunty sea-faring tunes, and the official welcoming party could be seen lined up on the pier beside them. Among them stood the Ambassador of Ireland to Japan, HE Padraig Murphy, Enterprise Ireland representative Declan Collins and Irish Navy Liaison Officer Lt Cdr Jim Shalloo. NIAMH was to berth ahead of a Japanese frigate, SAWAYUKI, its host ship for the visit, whose crew was lining the ship's side, the traditional sailor's greeting.

The first line ashore was greeted with a cheer from the people who had gathered on a walkway above the pier. The gangway followed, along which the first Irish naval personnel to disembark onto Japanese soil would shortly troop for the official arrival ceremony. The ceremony consisted of a parade made up of the ship's companies of NIAMH and SAWAYUKI, in the presence of Japanese and Irish dignitaries. They formed up on the pier, around a small podium. The Director of Tokyo Port Office, Yasuteru Yoshida, and Captain Kojima of SAWAYUKI addressed the parade. Mr Yoshida presented NIAMH's Captain with a shield to commemorate the first entry to the port by an Irish Navy ship. The Captain then addressed the parade. This ceremony was the ship's company's first exposure to the elegant Japanese custom of bowing, in greeting and in farewell, according acquaintances the correct degree of respect. It was suggested that NIAMH's Captain had been practising in his cabin, given the apparent ease with which he adapted to the custom. A presentation of beautiful Japanese flowers on behalf of Tokyo Port, followed by a flurry of press photographs, completed a warm welcome to this ancient and historic country.

NIAMH's Executive Officer, Lt Owen Mullowney, presided over a liaison meeting with his counterparts, while a lunch was hosted by the Captain onboard. In attendance were HE the Irish Ambassador, Rear Admiral Akahoshi, and Mr Yoshida of Tokyo Port. Following lunch, NIAMH's Captain and Commodore Kavanagh set off on the round of official calls of protocol, which included calls on the Chief of Staff of JMSDF, the Chairman of Joint Staff Council, the Minister for Defence, and the Administrative Vice Minister. A special greeting ceremony marked the arrival of Commodore Kavanagh at the Defence Agency HQ, which included a Guard of Honour. Later that afternoon, HE Ambassador Murphy and Commodore Kavanagh laid a wreath at a memorial to deceased

S/Lt Caoimhin MacUnfraigh,
Cadet Training Officer

Opposite page, crew from LE NIAMH visiting Shimofusa Naval Airbase

ABOVE LEFT, Honours Ceremony at
Japanese Defence Agency Headquarters
ABOVE RIGHT, Commodore John Kavanagh
and Admiral Ishihawa

members of the JMSDF.

Members of NIAMH's ship's company attended a reception on SAWAYUKI hosted by Admiral Kobayashi later that evening. It was a pleasant occasion and facilitated the first contact with the friendly and good-natured people of Japan. As this was this was the fifth Asian port to be visited, NIAMH's personnel were fully acclimatised to the use of chopsticks, and delighted in sampling the unique Japanese cuisine, with its emphasis on sushi and other fish delicacies.

On Tuesday, 9 April, 14 members of the ship's company were given a rare treat, visiting Shimofusa Naval Airbase, where they were given a detailed briefing on Japanese Maritime air patrol craft, and their training facilities. An opportunity to fly P3C Orion aircraft in simulation was included. They were then brought on a real version of the aircraft for an astounding flight around Tokyo city, its environs and, for good measure, out to sea.

Here, a few low level passes over some merchant ships on passage to Tokyo harbour were conducted.

Meanwhile, back onboard NIAMH, the work of promoting Ireland and Irish interests abroad had begun in earnest with a lunch hosted by Enterprise Ireland for business contacts. That evening, the first of several receptions, attended by 200 guests, was hosted onboard on behalf of IDA Ireland (the foreign direct investment agency of Ireland) and Tourism Ireland. The efforts of the crew had once again turned the flag deck from a grey metal ship's deck into an attractive garden, complete with grass green carpets, flowerpots and plants, traditional Irish music and fare. Credit here to Declan Collins of Enterprise Ireland for his procurement of the special green carpet, which enhanced the appearance and comfort of the reception area, and to Michael Gaffey, Counsellor at the Irish Embassy, who made all the protocol arrangements and organised the community events. Onboard talent

included flautist Cadet Niamh Ní Fhatharta, singer A/S Siobhan Fennell, ably supporting local Japanese musicians Isao and Masako Moriyasu (known as "Paddy" and "Brigid" in West Clare, where they are regular visitors), who provided musical entertainment, and Ms Choilfhionn Nic Fhearai, a 16-year-old exchange student from Dublin, who entertained guests at the Enterprise Ireland reception with Irish and classical compositions on the cello. The relative peace of the Tokyo evening was broken by the tones of L/S Frank Goss's bagpipes, as he saluted the 200 astonished Japanese guests with some stirring marching tunes. Following speeches by the Flag Officer, NIAMH's Captain, and HE Ambassador Padraig Murphy, everyone was encouraged to enjoy the evening, make some new friends, and engage in the traditional Japanese custom of ceremonially exchanging business cards. Traditional Irish fare served up by NIAMH's cooks was supplemented by delicious sushi, prepared onboard by local caterers.

On the following day, SAWAYUKI's Captain hosted lunch onboard for some of NIAMH's personnel, where more Japanese cuisine was enjoyed.

Later in the week, further lunches and receptions were hosted onboard NIAMH, on behalf of organisations such as Enterprise Ireland, Bord Bia (the Irish Food Board), Tourism Ireland, various Irish-based language schools under the auspices of MEI-RELSA, and companies in the IT sector. One such lunch was hosted on behalf of Shanahan Engineering, Blackrock, Co Dublin, whose MD, Liam Shanahan presented the ship with an inscribed Waterford Crystal ship's decanter.

As familiarity with Tokyo increased, more and more sightseeing was done, and reports of a fascinating city came back to the ship. The sightseeing had included tours of the Imperial Gardens, testament to the Japanese skill at tweaking nature into ever more wonderful shapes. Shrines in the city parks were also visited and some of the ship's

ABOVE LEFT, Commodore John Kavanagh presenting Defence Minister Nakatani with a Philip Gray painting
ABOVE RIGHT, local Japanese musicians Isao and Masako Moriyasu (also known as "Paddy" and "Brigid")

ABOVE LEFT, Takashi Toyama (1st left) and Liam Shanahan, MD, Shanahan Engineering (3rd left), with guests onboard NIAMH
ABOVE RIGHT, enthusiastic Tokyoites queue to visit LE NIAMH

company witnessed a traditional Japanese wedding ceremony. Tokyo Tower and the 55-floor Hyatt hotel, both affording wonderful views of Tokyo, were popular destinations as was the Olympic village, scene of the 1964 Olympics. The ship's company were by now old hands at the Tokyo nightlife scene, and those who were off duty after the onboard receptions, knew where to go to sample it. For many, the night kicked off in the reassuringly familiar surroundings of "Paddy Foleys Irish Bar" but, the scene having been set, many ventured to the clubs and discos, or to glimpse the more eccentric places that this city has to offer. Returning to the ship was better done in groups as the taxi fares were prohibitive and Tokyo's famous subway system doesn't run after midnight. It does however restart shortly after 5:00 am!

Meanwhile, the onboard duty watch looked after the security and safety of the ship, and tended to the ceremonial and diplomatic duties demanded of a naval ship

in port. On the afternoon on which the ship was open to the public, over 2,000 people visited NIAMH. The duty watch were kept busy as the crowds kept coming. Photographs were the order of the day, and giggling Japanese children were snapped sitting in the Captain's chair, while their parents toured the bridge, hungry for information on Ireland and the ship. It was a pleasant day, and presented the ship's company with an opportunity to meet Japanese people in an informal way. The following day's perusal of the Tokyo morning press showed that the efforts of NIAMH's tour guides had paid off as the ship's photograph appeared along with several articles. In fact, the Coxswain, CPO Martin Diggins, who appeared in one of the published photos was recognised on the street later that day because of it ... famous again!

Representatives of the Irish community were guests at the final reception. There are now over 1,300 Irish citizens resident in Japan, an extraordinary number for a country

ABOVE LEFT, A toast on board host ship SAWAYUKI
ABOVE RIGHT, Lt Commander O'Flynn takes his leave of host ship SAWAYUKI

of our size. They are a remarkable mix of people – priests and nuns who have devoted their lives to education in Japan, teachers of English, students, representatives of Irish companies, locally-based businesspeople and and even horse trainers and breeders. One elderly Sister's eyes filled with tears as she was told that she had just stepped aboard sovereign Irish territory – she had been teaching in Japan for the previous 40 years, without the chance of a return visit home.

Sunday, 14 April brought the opportunity for the cadets to visit their counterparts on the Japanese training ship KASHIMA. The cadets returned the favour later that day. That evening, Ambassador Murphy hosted a dinner attended by Admiral Ishikawa, the JMSDF Chief of Staff, other senior Japanese Admirals, Commodore Kavanagh, Declan Collins of Enterprise Ireland, and NIAMH's Captain.

Monday. 15 April, and the sad day of departure from

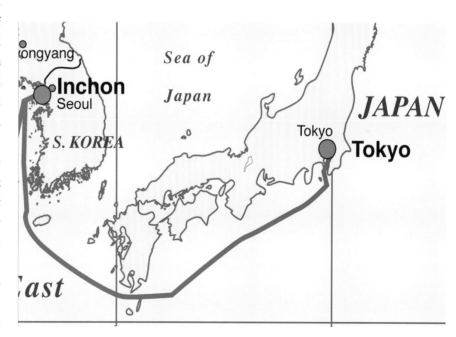

OPPOSITE PAGE TOP LEFT, Honour ceremony at the Japanese Defence Agency HQ
OPPOSITE PAGE TOP RIGHT, Welcome ceremony on arrival in Tokyo
OPPOSITE PAGE BOTTOM LEFT, Wreath laying at the Cenotaph
OPPOSITE PAGE BOTTOM RIGHT, Irish Ambassador HE Padraig Murphy with Commodore Kavanagh
RIGHT, CPO Martin Diggins enjoying sushi on board host ship SAWAYUKI
BELOW, Leaving Tokyo

Japan had arrived, 100 years almost to the day since the last visit of a Japanese naval ship to Ireland. The band of the JMSDF played NIAMH off the pier with some splendid renditions, and the crowd waved farewell as the last line was slipped. The Jack was struck, and NIAMH slipped slowly away under the by now familiar Rainbow Bridge.

A rendezvous had been arranged with the frigate SAWAYUKI for a final ceremony in Tokyo Bay. As the ships passed close by for the last time, ceremonial was exchanged, and both ship's companies raised their caps in salute, in honour of a warm and positive goodwill visit. A few "goodbye" toots on the ship's whistles marked the final farewell, as NIAMH set course for the South China Sea once more. Her next destination, Malaysia, 3,470 miles away – greater than the distance from Cork to Beirut, Lebanon.

Lafcadio Hearn

Patrick Lafcadio Hearn was born on Lefkas, Greece on 27 June 1850, the son of an Irish army doctor, Charles Hearn, and a Greek woman, Rosa Cassimati. He spent most of his youth in Ireland, completing his education in England. In his twenties, he discarded his first name, Patrick, and was known henceforth by his middle name, Lafcadio.

At the age of 19, Hearn went to America, where he found success as a journalist and writer. After two years in the West Indies, he went to Japan in 1890. He taught English in schools at Matsue and Kumamoto, in the south of the country. In 1896, he moved to Tokyo, where he taught at the Imperial University and, later, at Waseda University. He married Koizumi Setsu, a daughter of a *samurai*, and became a Japanese citizen, taking the name, Koizumi Yakumo.

Hearn write 13 books on Japan, providing a rich insight into his adopted country and making him arguably the most important Western interpreter of Japanese society and culture of that era. He died on 26 September 1904.

Lafcadio Hearn's works include: *Glimpses of Unfamiliar Japan; Out of the East; Kokoro; In Ghostly Japan; Shadowings; A Japanese Miscellany; Kwaidan; Japan: An Attempt at Interpretation.*

With thanks to HE Paul Murray, Irish Ambassador to Korea. For more information, see www.lafcadiohearn.jp.

JAPANESE NAVY CONNECTION WITH CORK

John and Cornelius Collins were born at Frenchfurze, Carrigaline, County Cork in 1851.

They served in the Royal Navy from 1865 to 1879 – as instructors to the Imperial Japanese Navy between 1873 and 1879. After they left the Royal Navy, they were invited by the Japanese Naval authorities to return to Japan as instructors. In total, they gave 15 years service to the Japanese Navy.

Both were conferred with the Sixth Class Order of the Rising Sun on 8 August 1888 by the Emperor Mei-relsaji.

The monument above in Carrigaline, County Cork was officially unveiled by the Japanese Ambassador to Ireland, His Excellency Kiyoshi Furukawa on 21 August 1994.

Japan

- Population: 126,771,662 (July 2002)
- Capital: Tokyo
- Port Visited by NIAMH: Tokyo
- Irish Ambassador: HE Pádraig Murphy
- Enterprise Ireland Manager for Japan: Declan Collins
- Enterprise Ireland clients active in Japan include:
  AEP Systems Ltd, Baltimore Technologies, Bank of Ireland International Services, Elan Corporation Ltd, Eontec, Euro Fish Products Ltd, eWare Ltd, Icon PLC, Iona Technologies PLC, Irish Distillers Ltd, Irish Dresden Ltd, Kerry Ingredients Ireland Ltd, Network365 Ltd, PARC Aviation Ltd, Parthus Ireland Ltd, Scientific Systems Ltd, Shanahan Engineering Ltd, SmartForce Ireland Ltd, Transware PLC, Waterford Wedgwood PLC, Xiam Ltd, Xsil Ltd.

Visit – Key Facts:
- Number of functions: 10
- Number of visiting decision-makers: 263
- Total number of visitors: 2620

CROSSING THE EQUATOR

Lt Owen Mullowney,
Executive Officer

On Monday, 15 April at 1525, LE NIAMH departed Tokyo Bay after an historic seven-day visit. Thoughts of the Equator were far from the crew's minds. But, several days of favourable weather and good progress meant that the possibility of "Crossing the Line" was becoming a reality. By Friday, the decision was taken that the ship would cross, and courses were plotted. In all, it added little more than 100 miles, or 6 hours steaming. However, preparations had to be made for the important ceremonial requirements of crossing the Equator for the first time.

Traditionally any members of a ship's company, who have not previously crossed the line, are initiated at a special ceremony, held to mark the occasion. On the day the Equator is crossed, one of the ship's company appears on the forecastle (front end of the ship) suitably attired as King Neptune, encrusted with barnacles, wearing a golden crown and flowing beard, and clasping a trident. The novices are then initiated by Neptune and receive a good ducking. This procedure earns them a certificate that exempts them from a repetition of the treatment on any future crossing of the line that they may undertake. The ceremony undoubtedly owes its origin to ancient pagan rites connected with the propitiation of the sea god Neptune (Poseidon, in Greek legend).

This tradition left NIAMH's crew with a problem, as nobody onboard had previously sailed across the Equator, so the traditional ceremony required some modification. Chief Petty Officer Owen O'Keefe as the oldest (if not the wisest) man

onboard was considered the ideal King Neptune. His wife, Queen Amphitrite normally accompanies King Neptune. With no females of a suitable age onboard (or acceptable males to play the role), Ordinary Seaman Sharon Darby assumed the role of Neptune's beautiful daughter, Ariel.

At 0830 on Monday 22 April, seven days after departing Tokyo, the crew mustered on the after deck as "15 minutes to crossing the line" was announced. It was a beautiful morning, clear sky and a bright sun that had risen just some two hours earlier. The temperatures were already in the 30s, and the sea was flat calm.

The ship's company mustered in their swimming gear, as King Neptune appeared suitably attired with crown, flowing beard, trident and – a unique Irish Navy tradition – a penguin on his shoulder! The assembled body grew excited at the sight of King Neptune, and the announcement of two miles to the equator. It was announced at 0846(H) on 22 April 2002, in position 105°26.7E, "Congratulations, everyone. You are members of the crew of the first Irish Naval vessel to cross the Equator". A loud cheer rang out. Congratulations were exchanged in recognition of achieving a feat that has been celebrated by sailors for hundreds of years

Engines were stopped one mile south of the equator, and the initiation ceremonies began. King Neptune was now firmly in charge and immediately summoned the Captain. A distinctly worried but wisely clad Captain was unceremoniously dragged in front of Neptune. Thriving in his new role, King Neptune made three demands of the Captain:

1. A shrubbery.
2. A modest sum of money from a member of the crew known for his thriftiness.
3. The youngest male virgin as a husband for his daughter.

The Captain was unable to accede to any of the demands. A furious King Neptune ordered his daughter Ariel to plaster the Captain with the prepared concoction. Neptune then ordered the Captain to walk the plank into the sea. Given the need for a thorough wash, and the possibility of escaping further censure, he was probably relieved to do so. The remainder of the ship's company soon followed in his wake, leaving a few hardy souls to mind the ship, and to tend King Neptune. With a seawater temperature of 32 degress, everybody quite enjoyed the swim. King Neptune himself was last into the water.

NIAMH had an arrival deadline to meet for Penang in Malaysia, and so the beautiful clear and warm waters of the Southern Hemisphere were soon abandoned as NIAMH set sail for a return to the Northern Hemisphere once again. So ended a unique chapter in the short but action-packed history of LE NIAMH. It is, and always will be, the first Irish Naval ship to "Cross the Line".

"Neptune" (CPO Owen O'Keefe) and his asssistant O/S Sharon Darby initiating NIAMH's Captain as the ship crosses the Equator

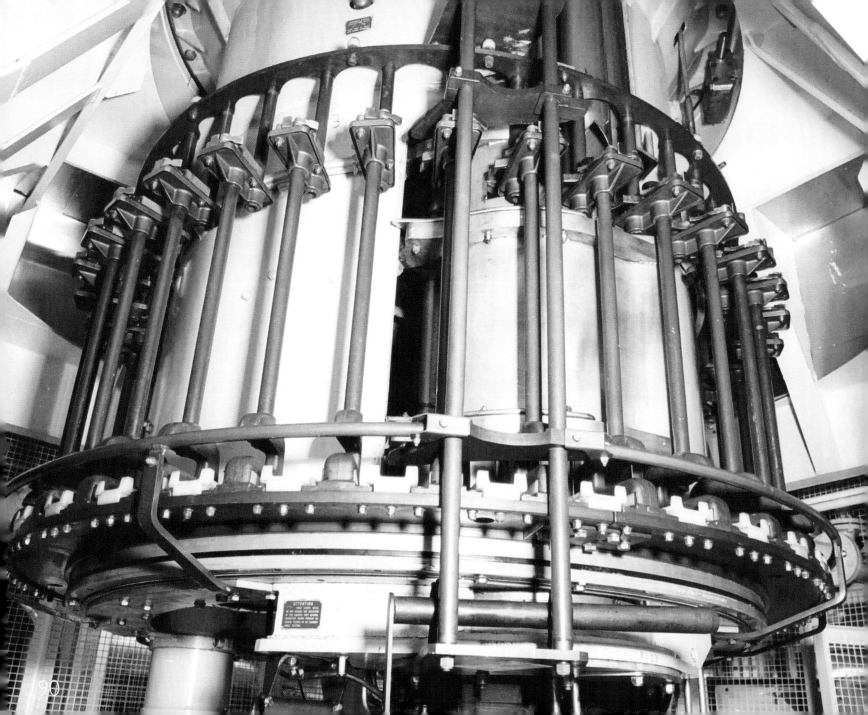

PENANG, MALAYSIA

LE NIAMH's departure from Penang, Malaysia on Sunday, 28 April marked the completion of the goodwill element of its historic visit to Asia. Ahead lay fuelling stops in Cochin, India, and Palma, Mallorca, a link-up with Irish UN troops in Massawa, Eritrea, a return passage through the Suez Canal, and a scheduled arrival at the Naval Base in Cork Harbour at 1235 on Tuesday, 21 May.

So was a Penang a success? NIAMH's ship's company would say "Yes", perhaps even "An overwhelming success" – but they would say that, wouldn't they? Nonetheless, there is some evidence to support the ship's company's claim.

On Saturday, 27 April when the ship was open to the public in Penang, over 3,000 people visited NIAMH. To cope with such numbers, local security had organised two queues – one at the gangway to the ship itself and one at the main entrance to the port, to join the queue at the gangway! There was major media interest in the visit. Over 40 journalists attended two separate press conferences. The visit was featured on national TV, and in all the main print media. Follow-up articles appeared in business and education journals.

The Chief Minister of Penang visited the ship, where he hosted a press conference, and signalled his support for the formation of an alumni association for Malaysian graduates of Irish Universities. The Tourism Minister attended a separate function onboard. The joy on the faces of the group of over 100 young children from a local orphanage, as they toured the ship wearing their newly-acquired LE NIAMH baseball caps, surely confirmed that the visit was going well.

On arrival in Penang, NIAMH was greeted by the Ambassador of Ireland to Malaysia HE Daniel Mulhall, local Enterprise Ireland representative, Corkman Anthony Courtney, accompanied by Michael Garvey, Enterprise Ireland's Director for Asia. The ship's Captain paid courtesy calls on the General Manager of Penang Port Commission, Dato'Captain HJ Abdul Rahim Abd Aziz; the President of the Town Council, Haji Mahadi Bin Mohb Ibrahim; and the Chief of Police, Datuk Arthur Edmond. The Chief of Police wondered whether anybody onboard NIAMH was related to a previous holder of his own office, a Commissioner O'Flynn, who held office from 1956 to 1962.

Following the calls of protocol, a press conference was held onboard NIAMH, where the media were briefed on Ireland's cultural and economic links with Malaysia. Ireland is the third largest EU exporter to Malaysia; Malaysia is Ireland's second most important Asian market after Japan, and third biggest market outside the EU. Despite the worldwide slow-down, the 2001 trade figures between Ireland and Malaysia increased by over 19% on the previous year, and were valued at almost €2 billion.

There is a strong educational link between Malaysia and

**Lt Commander Gerard O'Flynn,
Captain LE NIAMH**

OPPOSITE PAGE: The revolving feed of the ship's 76mm Oto Melara gun

ABOVE LEFT, The Hon Tan Sri Dr Koh Tsu Koon, Chief Minister being welcomed by Captain O'Flynn and Irish Ambassador HE Daniel Mulhall
ABOVE RIGHT, Anthony Courtney and Michael Garvey, Enterprise Ireland, with Dato Hj Shaik Ibrahim, Chairman, Nutrajaya Sdn Bhd, Irish Ambassador HE Daniel Mulhall and Lt Commander Anor Hj Jaffar

Ireland, with up to 1,000 Malaysians studying in Ireland at any one time. There has been a long tradition of Malaysian medical students attending the Royal College of Surgeons in Ireland (RCSI), in Dublin. Penang Medical College is a joint venture between the Penang State government, the Royal College of Surgeons in Ireland and University College Dublin. The Irish Universities and Medical Schools Consortium, which represents the colleges of the National University of Ireland, has a representative office in Malaysia. The consortium has recently extended its remit to recruiting Malaysian students for engineering and technological education, in addition to its traditional concentration on medicine. Malaysians represent the third biggest foreign grouping of students in Ireland. Distinguished Irish professors, such as Professor Tom Hennessy, Professor Noel Walsh, and Professor Dermot McDonald, who helped establish the Penang Medical College, attended a number of functions onboard NIAMH during its visit. With so many Malaysian graduates of Irish universities, the proposal to set up an Irish Universities Alumni Association was formally launched by

the Irish Ambassador HE Daniel Mulhall in the presence of the Chief Minister of Penang, Hon Tan Sri Koh Tsu Koon, at a special lunch held onboard. Over 100 guests, many of whom are graduates of the Royal College of Surgeons in Ireland, attended the event. The RCSI already has an Alumni Association, and its president Dato' Dr Godfrey Geh attended the function.

Some of the main Irish companies established in Malaysia include Kerry Ingredients, DATAC (remote technology), RCSI, ESBI (utilities & power generation), Softec (document management), FreightWatch International (security), the Irish Universities Medical Consortium (education promotion) and Microsol (software for utilities). It is a tribute to these and other companies that, between 2000 and 2001, Irish exports to Malaysia increased by 51%. The regard with which Irish companies are held in Malaysia is typified by remarks that a senior Malaysian businessman made in relation to Dr Denis Brosnan, Chairman and former CEO of Kerry PLC. He said that what impressed him most about Dr Brosnan was his focus on the long-term human resources situation, especially in relation to the future supply of

ABOVE LEFT, Lt Commander Gerard O'Flynn, Lt Commander Anor Hj Jaffar and Assistant Deputy Commander Chief of Police, Penang, Datuk Arthur Edmond
ABOVE RIGHT, Professor Tom Hennessy, Professor Kevin McDonald, Laura McDonald and Professor Noel McMahon, Penang Medical College

well-educated potential staff, and the availability of research staff and facilities, in sharp contrast to other international investors, whose principal focus seemed to be on short-term costs, and a quick return on investment.

On Thursday, 25 April, FreightWatch International and Dell Computers were co-hosted to dinner onboard. FreightWatch is an Irish security company focused exclusively on the logistics/distribution sector, and includes Dell among its high profile list of international clients. This young dynamic company includes among its staff several former members of the Defence Forces, including their general manager in Malaysia, Sean Henderson, who represented the company at the dinner and Mick Browne, general manager USA, a recently retired Irish Army officer, who served in the Army Ranger Wing. Dell Computers were represented by vice president John M Schaeffer, who had flown in specially for the function, and Jim Skelding, general manager for Malaysia, Singapore and India.

On Friday evening, a reception co-hosted by NIAMH's Captain and HE Ambassador Mulhall was attended by over 200

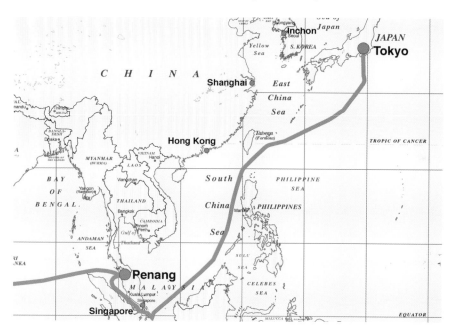

ABOVE LEFT, Malaysian visitors to LE NIAMH
ABOVE RIGHT, Anthony Courtney and
Michael Garvey, Enterprise Ireland, The Hon
Dato Kee Phaik Chen, State Minister for
Tourism, Penang, Mr Rizal Fauzi, and Ismail bin
Ahmad

guests, including Irish business connections, Irish business people, and graduates of the Irish education system.

On Saturday evening, NIAMH hosted a reception on behalf of two other companies with a strong presence in Malaysia: ESBI (ESB International) and Kentz. Given the quality of the singers that both companies include among their staff, it was fitting that the function should over-run slightly. The best rendition of the evening undoubtedly was "An Poc Ar Buile", including the launch of a verse in English. The singer however wishes to remain anonymous – careers have to be protected!

Ireland and Malaysia have been significant economic success stories over the last 20 years. Both countries recognise the value of investment in developing human resources and physical infrastructure. Both countries recognise the need for innovation in order to secure continued prosperity.

Education is the key to generating individuals with flair and innovation. The education system has helped forge strong links between Ireland and Malaysia. It is to be hoped that the visit of LE NIAMH to Penang has helped reinforce the strong links that already exist, and has created an increased awareness of the valuable trade links and opportunities that exist between both countries.

Malaysia

- Population: 22,229,040 (July 2001)
- Capital: Kuala Lumpur
- Port Visited by NIAMH: Penang
- Irish Ambassador: HE Daniel Mulhall
- Enterprise Ireland Manager for Malaysia: Tony Courtney (succeeded by Terry McParland, Autumn 2002)
- Enterprise Ireland clients active in Malaysia include: AEP Sytems Ltd, AHP Manufacturing BV, Aircraft Management Technologies Ltd, Am-Beo Ltd, Chameleon Colour Systems Ltd, Chanelle Veterinary Ltd, CR2 Ltd, DATAC Control Systems Ltd, Dublin Business School, Dublin City University, ESBI Computing, Electric Paper Company Ltd, Eurologic Systems Ltd, Irish Dairy Board, Kerry Ingredients Ltd, Medentech Ltd, Microsol Ltd, National University of Ireland Galway, Network365 Ltd, Nypro (Waterford) ltd, Park by Phone Ltd, PPI Adhesives Ltd, Royal College of Surgeons in Ireland, Selc Ireland Ltd, Sepro Telecom Intl Ltd, SIFCO Turbine Components Ltd, Sigma Wireless Technologies Ltd, SmartForce Ireland Ltd, Spectel Ltd, Tecpro Ltd, Trinity Biotech Mfg Ltd, Trintech Technologies, University College Cork, University College Dublin, University of Dublin Trinity College, Waterford Wedgwood PLC, Xiam Ltd.

Visit – Key Facts:
- Number of functions: 9
- Number of visiting decision-makers: 329
- Total number of visitors: 3085

detour to cross the Equator, was the longest non-stop passage of the whole deployment.

Penang (also known as Palua Pinang) consists of Penang Island, covering an area of 285 square kilometres, as well as Province Wellesley, 760 square kilometres in area on the mainland. The two locations are linked by Asia's longest bridge, the 13.5 kilometres-long Penang Bridge. The capital of Penang is Georgetown.

Malaysia is a multi-cultural society with a strong Muslim influence. Penang has a population of over one million people consisting of 32% Malays, 59% Chinese and 7% East Indian. English is widely spoken and understood by most. Bahasa Melayu is the national language, and other languages include Chinese and Tami. Penang was a British colony until 1957, when it gained independence and became one of the states of the newly-formed Federation of Malaya, which in 1963 became Malaysia. Penang gained further importance as a port in 1965, when Singapore ceded from Malaysia. In the 18th and 19th centuries, Penang was a major trading port specialising in tea, spices, china, and cloth.

Known as the Pearl of the Orient, Penang lies just off the west coast of peninsular Malaysia, and is 5 degrees North of the Equator (or some 300 miles). The nine-day passage from Tokyo, Japan, covering a distance of nearly 3,500 miles, including a slight

HOMECOMING

Tuesday, 21 May: 100 days after LE NIAMH, her captain and crew had set sail for Asia and the weather in Ireland hadn't changed one iota! Still wet, with stormy winds.

And, then, through the rain, a first glimpse of a grey shadow – LE NIAMH was home!

As she passed the houses and Cathedral of Cobh on her right, tug boats raced out to greet her, spraying their hoses in the air in a time-honoured tradition.

On the quayside at the Haulbowline Naval Dockyard, families, friends and naval staff gathered in the drizzle to welcome LE NIAMH.

There was a sincere and warm "Welcome Home" – "Fáilte ar ais go hÉireann" – from families and friends for the men and women who had achieved so much for Ireland in their 23,000 mile voyage. The formalities were few – the band of the Southern Brigade of the Irish Army played welcoming airs, while the Defence Force's Chief, Lt General Colm Mangan, the "Flag", Commodore John Kavanagh (who had travelled with NIAMH from Hong Kong to Tokyo), Enterprise Ireland's Peter Coyle, Michael Howard of the Department of Defense, Tony Joyce of the Department of Enterprise, Trade and Employment and Ken Thompson of the Department of Foreign Affairs were among the those who paid their respects to the ship's Captain, Gerard O'Flynn, in his quarters onboard NIAMH, which berthed alongside the Navy's flgship, LE EITHNE. Then it was a short walk across decks from NIAMH to EITHNE's helicopter hangar, where the crew and the families had gathered to shelter from the storm outside. The Captain thanked his crew and their ever-patient families, the Chief of Staff added his thanks and appreciation – and then it was all over. Asian Deployment 2002 had ended.

CADETS

An annual nationwide competition selects cadets to form the backbone of the officer corps in the Navy. These young people graduate from their course of training as Ensigns, with all the authority and responsibility of officer rank. The preparation they undergo to make the successful transition from young civilians to qualified naval officers is called a cadetship.

The naval cadetship is 24 months long. Candidates arrive on the Naval Base, Haulbowline in Cork Harbour, where they are given briefs on the various departments and duties of the Navy before proceeding to sea for an acquaint with a ship on patrol. They then move to the Defence Forces Training Centre in the Curragh, Co Kildare, where they undergo military training with their colleagues in the Army and the Air Corps. They build up their understanding of the military system and their place in it, learn basic military skills and bond with their colleagues in an atmosphere of demanding physical training and challenging academic work.

After their basic military training, cadets normally proceed to the Naval Base, Haulbowline for training geared towards preparing them for sea. Subjects include navigation and pilotage, seamanship, astro-navigation, fire fighting, damage control and naval gunnery. The aim of this stage is to equip the cadets with the basic professional and academic knowledge and skills essential to their immediate needs upon commissioning and their subsequent professional development.

The training must develop the cadets' character, personality and their qualities of leadership. A deep and motivating respect for truth, honour and loyalty, patriotism and courage, self-discipline and a sense of duty must be instilled. Every opportunity to fulfill this aim is taken. The Navy sought to include cadets on the Asian deployment of LE NIAMH because the trip crystallised many of these goals. It was fortuitous that the junior class were at a suitable stage of their training when NIAMH was deployed, because it was a golden opportunity to try their newly-acquired professional knowledge in a practical sphere. Two classes of cadets travelled on NIAMH: one group from Haulbowline to Hong Kong, the other from Hong Kong homewards.

For example, the trans-oceanic legs of the voyage provided them with the opportunity to carry out astro-navigation to a degree that is not possible at home given the frequently cloudy skies of our North Atlantic patrol area.

Being abroad in such exotic surrounds reinforced their understanding of what the Navy offers them as a career and assisted their bonding as a class. They were assessed in how they adapted to life onboard and, in particular, their leadership traits and socialisation skills were closely monitored. Seeing the ship and the reaction it received from Irish people abroad reinforced their understanding of their place in the world and the pride with which the ship was received and made them realise that they represent their country and their people when they present themselves abroad. The stiff requirements of the ship's diplomatic programme gave them an understanding of protocol while the requirement to be helpful, well turned out and sociable for the daily round of receptions and functions gave them an understanding of their role as hosts.

The ship drew on their individual talents in the area of sporting fixtures and music, which helped them to integrate with the ship's company. The fact that they were members of so cohesive a crew stood to them in the trials of their sea term (sea-time for junior cadets is always gruelling). It reinforced their *esprit de corp* and their sense of place within the Navy.

At sea, their twice-daily four-hour watch was supplemented by lectures in astro-navigation, which required them to be on the bridge at all hours for sightings. The engineering challenges posed by the high air and sea temperatures and the manner in which ship's personnel dealt with them gave the cadets an insight into the imaginative thinking frequently required in the Navy.

The cadets were told to prepare briefings on each port for the ship's company. These were then delivered before shore leave was granted and formed the basis of the crew's understanding of the area. All personnel, including the Captain, attended the briefings. The process of researching, preparing and delivering these briefs built up the cadets' confidence and public speaking ability.

The cadets also gained invaluable experience about the way in which the chain of command operates, not only from the point of

view of carrying out operations and exercises abroad but also how to deal with the inevitable personnel issues that arise on such a long deployment to such a far-away place.

Overall, their inclusion on NIAMH's trip allowed the cadets to be closely monitored and assessed. It built up their own confidence and their understanding of their role. It allowed them to practice the skills that they had learned in the classroom and it taught them much about life in the Navy. The trip was an education for them and a spur to their further development.

REFLECTIONS AFTER THE EVENT

In order to evaluate fully the success of the promotional mission during LE NIAMH's visit to Asia, Enterprise Ireland commissioned Drury Research to conduct research with a sample of attendees at various events.

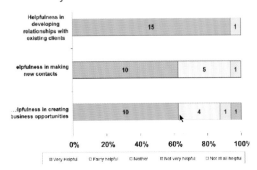

The attendees surveyed included Irish company and agency executives in Ireland, China, Japan, Malaysia and Australia. The sectors included were engineering (4), education and language (5), IT (3), fisheries (1), distribution (1), tourism (1) and the food sector (1). Half (8) of the sixteen companies surveyed had attended one event onboard LE NIAMH, four had attended two events, with the remaining four attending three events.

Across all sectors, there was general agreement that the unique appeal of this novel platform encouraged the target audience (key individuals) to attend and participate in events associated with the mission. Overall, attendees were very positive towards the contribution that the mission made both to their business and to their relationships with Asian clients. Most companies found the mission helpful for making new contacts. For a minority of Irish companies, a number of the event locations (for example, Korea) were also new business markets and therefore presented an opportunity to make a notable first impression on potential clients in such regions. All organisations interviewed agreed that the events attended were successful in securing new business or retaining existing clients for their company. All sixteen interviewees were satisfied with the event and fourteen awarded the event their highest rating (very satisfied).

Enterprise Ireland and the Department of Foreign Affairs were commended several times for their organisation of the events. The Irish Ambassadors involved were also mentioned with appreciation. LE NIAMH's crew were also praised for contributing to the successful delivery of the event, with many participants paying tribute to the "magnificent ambassadors for Ireland".

TOP GRAPH: Perceived helpfulness of event
MIDDLE GRAPH: Was participation helpful in securing new business
BOTTOM GRAPH: Satisfaction with organisation, management and delivery

Not only was Asian Deployment 2002 the single longest and most challenging mission undertaken by the Irish Navy, it also represented the most complex, far-flung and ambitious trade mission ever mounted by Enterprise Ireland for its clients.

Seven ports in six countries in just over seven weeks, of which sailing time accounted for almost half. Thirty-three business-related events were held onboard LE NIAMH, with 2,411 key business and government figures in attendance. Thirty-three Irish companies and agencies were represented on the trade mission, almost half of them hosted a dedicated event onboard, with some of them involved in more than one event. Clearly, a successful gathering of business potential in a unique setting, more than achieving the targets set.

In addition, a further 881 media and other officials attended functions onboard and LE NIAMH received visits from over 7,000 members of the public or from Irish families living in Asia.

An independent market research firm, engaged by Enterprise Ireland and the Navy, to survey the companies that took part in the trade mission, found a very positive reaction. Almost all the companies found the events "very helpful" in developing relationships with existing clients and most found it "very helpful" also in making new contacts or in creating business opportunities. Several reported new contract signings with new and existing clients following events. But dry statistics, even when illustrated with charts, can only tell part of the story. Perhaps the participants should speak for themselves.

During the LE NIAMH Asian tour, DATAC took the opportunity to unveil its state-of-the-art Navigator RTU monitoring device to the marine departments of Singapore, Malaysia and Hong Kong. Considerable interest was shown in the Navigator and we expect follow-on sales as a result of the exhibition platform afforded by the LE NIAMH visit.

Ray O'Flaherty
Sales Manager
DATAC Control
International Ltd

The professionalism of the Irish Navy, the efficient organisation by Enterprise Ireland, together with the excellent facilities onboard LE Niamh, allowed BIM to promote and develop the awareness and profile of Irish seafood in a manner that was totally appropriate to the markets concerned.

Helen Brophy
Market Development
Manager
Bord Iascaigh Mhara

The FreightWatch Group's aim in participating in the LE NIAMH trade mission was to reciprocate hospitality in a traditional Irish way to key clients and potential clients. The presence of the LE NIAMH in Penang, and the opportunities it presented in having a Captain's Dinner onboard, enabled FreightWatch Group to promote ourselves, our services and our nationality in an environment where clients and potential clients were relaxed and at ease. We believe that the evening was a success and augurs well for our continued success in the region.

Shaun Henderson
General Manager
FreightWatch Malaysia Sdn
Bhd

Our aim in participating in the LE NIAMH trade mission was to launch our Singapore office in a unique way while highlighting our Irish heritage. The event was extremely successful for us. The novelty of attending an office opening on board an Irish Naval vessel ensured we had an enthusiastic and large attendee list. The professionalism, charm, friendliness and humour of the crew were a wonderful reflection of Ireland and IONA. Thank you to all concerned!

Majella Nolan
Marketing Manager - ASEAN
IONA Technologies Asia
Pacific Pty Ltd

A wonderful platform for making new contacts and renewing old ones. The atmosphere of the LE NIAMH provided by the Irish Navy was one of typical Irish "Céad Míle Fáilte" and provided friends from abroad the opportunity to experience doing business in a friendly, personalised way. The EFL industry in Ireland has developed so much over the past few years and has broadened its scope to include many new distant markets. We certainly achieved that which we set out to do, which was to initiate new business and renew old contacts. Having been part of the trip to China, Korea and Japan, I can only say that it was a huge success and great credit is due to Enterprise Ireland for such an innovative idea.

Grainne Barton
Director
The Linguaviva Centre Ltd

ESB INTERNATIONAL

THE FOOD ISLAND

The visit of the LE NIAMH was an excellent way to combine Irish hospitality with a unique and interesting venue to promote Irish business in the region.

Roy Lauder
Regional Manager Asia-Pacific
ESB International

The visit of the LE NIAMH provided a first class context within which Shanahan was able to consolidate existing relationships, as well as successfully lay the foundations for new business development.

Geoff Porter
Manager - Business Development
Shanahan Engineering Ltd.

Bord Bia clients were very honoured to be invited on board the LE NIAMH during its visit to Asia. The friendliness and hospitality of the crew projected a very warm and positive image of Ireland.

Frank Murray
International Markets
Bord Bia

The Irish Business Forum of Hong Kong was delighted to have the opportunity to arrange cocktails for its members and guests on board the LE NIAMH during its week-long stay in Victoria Harbour. The weather was kind to us and the Captain, officers and crew were tremendous hosts for the evening with generous servings of food and drink. Over 80 attended including representatives of all of the member chambers and business associations of the European Chamber of Commerce in Hong Kong, of which the IBF is a member. Noel Davern TD, Minister of State for the Department of Agriculture, Food & Rural Development was the guest of honour. The visit truly raised the profile of Ireland and the Irish community in Hong Kong and the IBF would welcome further visits and initiatives by the Irish Government of this nature.

Mervyn Jacob
President
Irish Business Forum of Hong Kong

BELOW, Ian Crowhurst, Gaelic Inns, Hugh Hoyes-Cock and Yasmine of O'Brien's Sandwich Bars
OPPOSITE PAGE, The control panel for loading the ship's 76mm Oto Melara gun

Overall, LE NIAMH's visit received significant – and favourable – radio, TV and print media coverage prior to and during the stop-overs in the various ports. This helped to raise both Ireland's profile generally and that of Irish exporters into the region.

The Captain and his crew excelled themselves as ambassadors for Ireland and made many friends in Asia, thus helping to further Ireland's Asian connections. All those who were privileged to be associated with the NIAMH voyage to Asia in 2002 will long hold the memory of that extraordinary series of events.

A SUCCESSFUL MISSION

Editor, Brian O'Kane, interviews Peter D Coyle, Executive Director, Enterprise Ireland for his conclusions on the success of the trade mission.

BOK: NIAMH has returned home, her crew has rested and the ship herself has returned to her normal routine patrolling off the Irish coast. Sufficient time has passed now to allow impressions and views of the voyage to Asia to be seen in perspective. Was it worthwhile? Should we do it again?

PDC: The answer to the first question is a resounding "Yes". The statistics gathered by Enterprise Ireland and the Navy throughout the voyage show that the objective – attracting 2,000+ Asian government and business decision-takers onboard NIAMH – was handsomely exceeded. A total of 2,411 decision-takers attended functions on the ship, along with a further 881 media and other officials. In fact, well over 10,000 people visited NIAMH during 62 events, 34 of which were specifically associated with business and, thus, Enterprise Ireland's work. The vast majority of those interviewed by an independent market research firm after the mission stated that the events they had been involved with onboard NIAMH had contributed strongly to their business in Asia: New contacts were made, existing business relationships were cemented and, indeed, in some instances, actual deals were concluded. A typical comment from an Irish executive was "I thought it was well run, well executed, well targeted and extremely successful, overall an extremely well run affair". You can't get much better than that!

BOK: What was the secret of the trade mission's success?

PDC: The use of a Navy vessel for promotional purposes was particularly apt for the target audience. "Asian guests felt important being invited ... onboard a naval ship to attend an official Government event and to meet the Ambassador", one executive told us. Almost everyone interviewed was satisfied with the events staged, the administration and so on. And, in particular, there was a lot of positive comment about the professionalism, friendliness and positive attitude of the crew on NIAMH. This was key.

BOK: So, should we do it again?

PDC: All of the executives surveyed said that they would be likely to use a platform such as NIAMH again and would welcome a similar mission based on a Navy vessel taking place every one to two years. But not every overseas trip by a Navy vessel can, or should, have a business or, indeed, a diplomatic, dimension to it. In particular, the issue of resources must be borne in mind. Voyages such as that of NIAMH to Asia cost a lot of money and, also, have a high opportunity cost, in that a patrol vessel is taken away from normal duties. The small Irish Navy, as I have discovered, has a demanding work programme.

So, before setting out the Enterprise Ireland stall, so to speak, I must emphasise that, ultimately, decisions about the deployment of Navy vessels are reserved to the Minister for Defence who must balance difficult issues of resources, especially the need for patrol-time off the Irish coast, with the demands of agencies such as Enterprise Ireland. Our view is that future voyages such as that undertaken to Asia by NIAMH – major deployments that have business, trade and diplomacy as their prime purpose – should be focussed either on areas where Ireland has a low profile but the opportunities are great or on areas where there are opportunities but where Ireland's international trade image requires burnishing. Against that backdrop, our view is that, over the next number of years,

consideration might be given to undertaking a repeat visit to Asia and perhaps extending this to Australia as well, while South Africa and the Great Lakes areas of North America (specifically, the cities of Montreal, Toronto and Chicago) should also be on the list. And, when their economies recover, it might be worthwhile visiting a number of Latin American locations.

Peter D Coyle, Executive Director - Asia, Enterprise Ireland congratulates Lt Commander Gerard O'Flynn, Captain LE NIAMH on completion of a successful mission

PROVEN CAPABILITY!

**Commander Mark Mellett,
Plans and Policy Unit,
Naval Headquarters**

In an interview with the Editor, Commander Mark Mellett, Plans and Policy Unit, Naval Headquarters comments on the outcome of the LE NIAMH Asia Deployment from a Navy perspective.

BOK: *It's clear that NIAMH's mission to Asia was a great success. Commander Mellett, from the Navy viewpoint, what is the significance of that success?*

MM: For the Defence Forces, the deployment was of major significance. At a national level, it clearly demonstrated the utility of the Navy as an instrument to further diplomatic, economic, cultural and indeed military interests on the other side of the world. Before the deployment, to suggest that Ireland had the capacity for independent global reach within its Defence Forces would at the very least have been greeted with raised eyebrows. Now, it can be taken as a given.

BOK: *But was there not a huge risk for the Defence Forces in undertaking the mission? What if it had gone wrong?*

MM: Yes, for the Defence Forces, there was no fall-back position. The risk was borne by the Navy once it assured the Minister that the deployment was within its capacity. And so, from a strategic perspective, the deployment not only exercised the planning capacity of the Forces but, more importantly, proved that capacity

for this and similar type service delivery.

There can be no doubt that LE NIAMH boxed above her weight. Credit is due to her Commanding officer and crew, who did a remarkable job. By international standards, she is a small ship and, as such, was restricted in the time of year she could undertake the mission and in the level of service she could accommodate in the mission area. Indeed, most of the stakeholders felt additional space onboard would have been beneficial and this will be a consideration when planners come to decide on the next generation of patrol vessels.

BOK: *What has the Navy learnt from the Asia Deployment?*

MM: With a marine designated area of almost one million square kilometres, there is a strong case to invest in Naval vessels to help further our national interests in the waters where Ireland has sovereign rights – our basic service role. But the Asia deployment has helped to fashion a new perspective on the utility of Naval vessels for duties beyond our immediate home waters.

Ireland is an island in a rapidly changing world. To get the most from its limited resources, it will need to be smarter and faster in the way it reacts to regional and global changes in all areas – economic, security, diplomatic and humanitarian. The government recognises the unique characteristics of Naval vessels as an expression of State sovereignty and political will at sea and in furthering such policy objectives in the international maritime domain. Accordingly, planners must be conscious of this recognition in the context of the future development of the Navy.

The Navy does not exist just to provide basic service delivery requirements. It is in times of crisis – or opportunity – whether environmental, security, diplomatic or even military – that society rightly expects the Navy to perform a broader range of functions in the maritime domain that are vital to the nation's well-being. In the aftermath of the Asia deployment, the Navy stands in good stead because it has proved it can do just that!

FACTS AND FIGURES

Asian ports visited:

During the goodwill visit, seven ports were visited as follows:

- Singapore
- Hong Kong
- Shanghai
- Incheon
- Tokyo
- Penang
- Cochin.

LE NIAMH delivered supplies to the Irish troops stationed in Eritrea with the UN Forces, and a number of re-fuelling stops were also made *en route* to Asia and on the return voyage.

Functions:

- Total number of events held on board during the goodwill mission: 62
- Total number of events specifically associated with business: 34

In addition, in each of the seven ports visited on the goodwill mission, a general reception was held and the Captain hosted events for the Port Authorities in each port.

Visitors to the ship:

Business:	1,603
Government:	808
Others – Press, etc:	881
Members of the Public, local Irish families, etc:	7,110
Total:	10,402

This number excludes the crew and Captain of LE NIAMH, as well as the Irish Ambassador, Embassy and Enterprise Ireland staff in each port visited.

Front row (L to R), Minister for Health, Michael Martin TD, Flag Officer Commodore John Kavanagh, Dr Martin McAleese, HE President of Ireland Mary McAleese, Chief of Staff Irish Defence Forces Lt General Colm Mangan, Peter D Coyle, Executive Director - Asia, Enterprise Ireland, with members of the crew of LE NIAMH

LE NIAMH'S CREW

Officer Commanding	Lt Cdr	Gerard O'Flynn
Executive Officer	Lt	Owen Mullowney
Gunnery Officer	S/Lt	Eric Timon
Marine Engineering Officer	Lt Cdr	Michael Malone
Navigation Officer	S/Lt	Roberta O'Brien
Coxswain	CPO	Martin Diggins
Chief Engine Room Artificer	CPO	Owen O'Keeffe
Senior Petty Officer Supplies	SPO	John Duffy
Boatswain	PO	Niall Dunne
PO/Engine Room Artificer	PO	Stephen Bruton
PO/Engine Room Artificer	PO	Patrick O'Donnell
PO/Engine Room Artificer	PO	Adrian O'Meara
PO/Electrician	PO	Dean Victory
PO/Mechanician	PO	Joseph Morrison
PO/Cook	PO	Brendan Moriarty
PO/Steward	PO	Thomas Lowry
PO/Tel	PO	Cronan Doyle
PO/Radio Radar Technician	PO	Stephen O'Leary
L/Seaman	LS	Nicholas Murphy
L/Seaman	LS	Paul Shanahan
L/Seaman	LS	Paul Patterson
L/Emergency Medical Technician	LS	James Byrne
L/Cook	LS	Alan Ferguson
L/Steward	LS	Frank Goss
Seaman	O/Sea	Sharon Darby
Seaman	A/Sea, DSM	Gerard Dore
Seaman	A/Sea	Kevin Heade
Seaman	A/Sea	Padraig O'Flynn
Seaman	O/Sea	Siobhan Fennell
Seaman	O/Sea	Paul O'Shea
Seaman	A/Sea	Fergus Blackmore
Mechanician	A/Me	Keith Mallon
Mechanician	A/Me	Gerard Cunningham
Mechanician	A/Me	Patrick Garvey
Mechanician	O/Me	John O'Driscoll

Electrician	A/EA	Kieran Conroy
Communications Operator	A/Com Op	Simon Pollard
Communications Operator	A/Com Op	Finola Lafferty
Communications Operator	A/Com Op	Victoria Kelly
Steward	A/Stw	Stacey Tait
Cook	A/Ck	Michael O'Keeffe

HONG KONG TO TOKYO

Flag Officer	Comdre	John Kavanagh

HAULBOWLINE TO HONG KONG, OUTBOUND

Cadet Training Officer	Lt	Cathal Power
Cadet	Cdt	Dominic Kelly
Cadet	Cdt	David Lyons
Cadet	Cdt	Paul Hegarty
Cadet	Cdt	Elaine Browne
Cadet	Cdt	Catriona Walsh
Cadet	Cdt	David Fleming

HONG KONG TO HAULBOWLINE, RETURN

Cadet Training Officer	S/Lt	C Mac Unfraigh
Cadet	Cdt	Stewart Donaldson
Cadet	Cdt	Niamh Ni Fhatharta
Cadet	Cdt	Grace Fanning
Cadet	Cdt	Thomas Brunicardi
Cadet	Cdt	David O'Rourke

HONG KONG

RC Naval Chaplain	Rev Fr	Desmond Campion, CF

PORT LIAISON OFFICERS

Liaison Officer	Cdr, DSM	Mark Mellett
Liaison Officer	Lt Cdr	James Shalloo

ENTERPRISE IRELAND

ENTERPRISE IRELAND OFFICES IN ASIA

EXECUTIVE DIRECTOR,
responsible for Asia
(based in Dublin):
Peter D Coyle
Peter.Coyle@
enterprise-ireland.com

DIRECTOR ASIA:
(based in Hong Kong)
Michael Garvey
Michael.Garvey@
enterprise-ireland.com

CHINA
Manager: Alan Hobbs

Beijing
Enterprise Ireland
c/o Commercial Section Embassy of Ireland
C612A Office Building, Beijing Lufthansa Centre
No. 50 Liangmaqiao Road
Chaoyang District
Beijing 100016, CHINA

Contact: Alan Hobbs
Email: Alan.Hobbs@enterprise-ireland.com
Li.Bo@enterprise-ireland.com
Jenny.Zhang@enterprise-ireland.com
Tel: +86 10 8448 8080
Fax: +86 10 8448 4282

Shanghai
Enterprise Ireland
Commercial Section
Consulate General of Ireland
Suite 700A Shanghai Centre
1376 Nanjing Road West
Shanghai 200040, CHINA

Contact: Renee Wu
Email: Renee.Wu@enterprise-ireland.com
Tel: +86 21 6279 7088
Fax: +86 21 6279 7066

Hong Kong
Enterprise Ireland
2107, Tower 2, Lippo Centre
89 Queensway, Hong Kong

Contact: Patrick Yau
Email: Patrick.Yau@enterprise-ireland.com
Wansey.Li@enterprise-ireland.com
Tel: + 852 2845 1118
Fax: + 852 2845 9240

MIDDLE EAST & WEST ASIA
(including India)
Manager: Nick Marmion

Dubai
Enterprise Ireland.
PO Box 62425, Gulf Business Centre
Crowne Plaza Commercial Tower
Sheikh Zayed Road
Dubai, United Arab Emirates

Contact: Nick Marmion
Email: Nick.Marmion@enterprise-ireland.com
Tel: + 971 4 332 4025
Fax: + 971 4 332 8860

Riyadh
Enterprise Ireland
C/o Embassy of Ireland
PO Box 94349
Riyadh 11693, Saudi Arabia

Contact: Ikram UrRehman
Email: Ikram.UrRehman@enterprise-ireland.com
Tel: +966 1 488 1383
Fax: +966 1 488 1094

MALAYSIA /THAILAND/ VIETNAM
Manager: Terry McParland

Kuala Lumpur
Enterprise Ireland
Ireland House
5th Floor South Block, The Amp Walk
218 Jalan Ampang
50450 Kuala Lumpur
Malaysia

Contact: Terry McParland
Email: Terry.McParland@enterprise-ireland.com
Sabrina.Ng@enterprise-ireland.com
Tel: +60 3 2164 0616/8
Fax: +60 3 2164 0619

SINGAPORE (plus Philippines)
Manager: KB Lim

Singapore
Enterprise Ireland
541 Orchard Road, 8th Floor
Liat Towers
Singapore 238881

Contact: KB Lim
Email: KB.Lim@enterprise-ireland.com
Judy.Chan@enterprise-ireland.com
Tel: +65 6733 2180
Fax: +65 6733 0291

AUSTRALIA (Plus New Zealand)
Manager: Anne Casey

Sydney

Enterprise Ireland
Level 30, 400 George Street
Sydney, NSW 2000
Australia

Contact: Anne Casey
Email: Anne.Casey@enterprise-ireland.com
Craig.Lowe@enterprise-ireland.com
Tel: +612 8233 6214
Fax: +612 9231 6769

JAPAN (plus Korea)
Manager: Declan Collins

Tokyo

Enterprise Ireland
Ireland House 1F
2-10-7, Kojimachi
Chiyoda-ku
Tokyo 102-0083
Japan
Contact: Declan Collins
Email: Declan.Collins@enterprise-ireland.com
Takashi.Toyoma@enterprise-ireland.com
Reiko.Hiruma@enterprise-ireland.com
Michie.Kusakari@enterprise-ireland.com
Mika.Utsugi@enterprise-ireland.com
Tel: +81 3 32630611
Fax: +81 3 32630614

Korea

Enterprise Ireland
15th Floor, Daehan Fire & Marine Insurance B/D
51-1 Namchang-Dong, Chung-Ku
Seoul 100-778
Korea

Contact: Meejung Lee
Email: idaseoul@kornet.net
Tel: + 82 2 755 4767/8
F: + 82 2 757 3969

ACKNOWLEDGEMENTS

The execution of a voyage as complex as that of LE NIAMH's Asian Deployment would not be possible without the enthusiastic co-operation and involvement of a great many organisations and individuals.

The Voyage

Government Departments and agencies that had a substantial involvement in making the mission successful were:

- Department of Defence, incorporating the Defence Forces and the Navy
- Department of Enterprise, Trade and Employment, incorporating Enterprise Ireland and the Asia-Pacific Strategy Committee
- Department of Foreign Affairs, including the Irish Embassies in Asia.

Other Government Agencies that were involved in the mission were:
- Bord Bia (the Irish Food Board)
- Bord Iascaigh Mhara (the Irish Fisheries Board)
- IDA Ireland
- Tourism Ireland.

Irish companies that provided supplies in some form to the ship for the voyage included:
- Bailey's
- Bord Bia
- Bord Iascaigh Mhara
- Cooley Distilleries
- Dairygold, owners of Blarney Mineral Water
- Football Association of Ireland
- Guinness
- Heineken
- Irish Dairy Board
- Irish Rugby Football Union
- Kerry PLC
- Waterford Wedgwood PLC.

The Captain of LE NIAMH, Lt Commander Gerard O'Flynn, the Navy and Enterprise Ireland wish to express their appreciation to all concerned.

The Book

ASIAN ENTERPRISE: LE NIAMH's Goodwill Voyage to Asia 2002 has been compiled from a wide range of sources to whom the Editor wishes to express his grateful appreciation, including:

- A/S David Jones, photographer, Irish Navy
- Anthony Courtney and Declan Collins, Enterprise Ireland
- Captain Kojima, Japanese host ship, SAWAYUKI, for photographs
- Commander Mark Mellett, Plans and Policy Unit, Naval Headquarters, Naval Service, for text and guidance
- Daichi Fukushima, for use of material from www.lafcadiohearn.jp
- Defence Forces Press Office, especially Commandant Ciaran McDaid, for guidance and for facilitating access to Navy personnel
- Department of Defence, for permission to reproduce material from its publications and website
- Harry O'Neill, Irish Business Forum of Hong Kong, for an ex-patriate's perspective
- Hugh Tully, Navy Press Officer, for assistance and contacts
- Industrial Interfaces, for the cutaway drawings of LE NIAMH
- Irish Ambassador to Korea, HE Paul Murray, for text
- Japanese Maritime Self-Defence Force, for photographs
- John Coleman of La Tene Maps, for maps of LE NIAMH's voyage
- Lee Video Productions Sdn Bhd, Penang, Malaysia, for use of photographs
- LE NIAMH's Bosun, PO Niall Dunne, for photographs
- LE NIAMH's Cadet David Fleming, for text
- LE NIAMH's Cadet Dominic Kelly, for text
- LE NIAMH's Cadet Training Officer, Lt Caoimhin Mac Unfraigh, for text
- LE NIAMH's Cadet Training Officer, Lt Cathal Power, for text
- LE NIAMH's Captain, Lt Commander Gerard O'Flynn, for text, photographs and his always courteous "steer"
- LE NIAMH's Communications Operator, A/Com Op, Victoria Kelly, for text
- LE NIAMH's Executive Officer, Lt Owen Mullowney, for text and photographs
- LE NIAMH's Gunnery Officer, S/Lt Eric Timon, for text and photographs
- LE NIAMH's Marine Engineering Officer, Lt Commander Michael Malone, for text and photographs
- LE NIAMH's Navigation Officer, S/Lt Roberta O'Brien, for text
- Lt Commander Jim Shalloo, Plans and Policy Unit, Naval Headquarters, Naval Service, for text and guidance
- Marie Kearns, photographer, Enterprise Ireland

- Michael Garvey, Director - Asia, Enterprise Ireland for fact-checking
- Peter D Coyle, Executive Director, Enterprise Ireland, for his encouragement in the "Asian Enterprise" book project from the start
- Philip Gray, Irish artist, for permission to use his painting "Asian Odyssey" for the cover
- Takeshi Sera, photographer, Tokyo, Japan, for use of photographs
- Thomas Choong, photographer, Singapore, for use of photographs.

In addition, a special "Thank You" to Jackie FitzGerald and Siobhan Curley of Enterprise Ireland for their seamless co-ordination of the many arms of the publishing project.

Publication of **ASIAN ENTERPRISE: LE NIAMH'S Goodwill Voyage to Asia 2002** has been made possible by generous sponsorship from:
- Bord Iacaigh Mhara
- Bord Bia
- DATAC Control International Ltd
- ESBI
- FreightWatch
- IDA Ireland
- Intuition Publishing
- Iona Technologies
- MEI-RELSA
- Shanahan Engineering
- Tourism Ireland.

R&A Bailey & Co.

Bailey's is Ireland's leading export spirit brand. It is the world's No.1 liqueur and the 9th largest selling premium spirit brand worldwide. It is the single most successful new product to be launched in the drinks industry in the past 30 years. The demand for Bailey's in 130 countries worldwide is served entirely from Ireland and represents over 50% of all Irish spirits exports. Over 50,000 gallons of milk are used in its making and last year the company sold 5.7 millon cases, (some 68.4 million bottles), representing a 10% growth on the previous year. This double digit growth is set to continue, with demand projected to take sales to 10 million 9 ltr. cases by 2007 or sooner. In response, the company has invested 64 million Euro in a second site, in Northern Ireland which will come on stream next summer. R&A Bailey & Co. is a Diageo company.

Bord Bia (the Irish Food Board)
www.bordbia.ie

Bord Bia's corporate vision is "To champion the success of Irish food and drink" and our mission is to "deliver effective and innovative market development, promotion and information services for our clients". Our focus is the export market. We use our logo - inspired by Ireland's green, natural landscape, enriched by nature's purest ingredient, the raindrop - to promote a positive image of Irish food and drink worldwide.

Bord Iacaigh Mhara (the Irish Fisheries Board)
www.bim.ie

The visit of LE Niamh presented an opportunity to BIM to support its ongoing marketing initiatives in Asia. Since the mid-1970s, Asia, in particular, the Japanese market, has been of substantial importance to the Irish seafood sector. Herring roe, mackerel and horse mackerel are the main products exported to the Japanese market, which stands as Ireland's most important non-EU market at a current value of over €20 million per annum. In addition, the Chinese, Hong Kong and Korean markets are of significant importance for other types of seafood products, including shellfish and salmon. The visit of the LE Niamh was a professional and integrated approach to targeting potential and existing customers. BIM's activities during the visit were well received and have led to a number of opportunities for participating companies.

DATAC Control International Ltd
www.datac-control.com

DATAC is an Irish company involved in the design, manufacture and installation of telemetry and SCADA systems for remote monitoring and control. Headquartered in Dublin, Ireland, DATAC has 80 employees worldwide, with four based in Malaysia, Brunei, United Arab Emirates and Hong Kong. Export sales to Asia totalled US$7million over the last five years. The Malaysian Marine Department is a client, and the Water Supplies Department of Hong Kong has been a customer for nearly 20 years, as result of which DATAC's software and hardware control the distribution of over 65% of the territory's drinking water supply.

Department of Defence
www.irlgov.ie/defence

The mission of the Department is to contribute to national security and stability by the provision of Defence Forces capable of fulfilling the roles assigned by government and to provide an effective civil defence capability. The work of the Department involves a range of policy, planning, legislative and administration activities in relation to defence policy generally; Defences Forces organisation, regulation and control, recruitment and training, conciliation and arbitration, pay and allowances, conditions and superannuation, and purchase of stores and equipment. The Department is responsible also for the general planning, organisation and co-ordination of civil defence measures, including special guidance for local authorities. The Department plays a key role in providing aid to the civil power, mainly in the area of security, fishery protection, search and rescue and air emergency services, government air transport and international peacekeeping.

Department of Enterprise Trade & Employment
www.entemp.ie
The Department is charged with the implementation and development of government policy in the areas of enterprise, employment promotion, trade development, the regulation of businesses and the protection of workers. Detailed responsibilities are: industrial development policy, science and technology, company and patents law, regulation of insurance companies and friendly societies, control of mergers, distributive trade legislation, trade policy and trade promotion, consumer protection, industrial relations and various matters affecting the conditions of employment of workers including occupational safety, health and welfare.

Department of Foreign Affairs
www.gov.ie/iveagh/
The Department of Foreign Affairs advises the Minister for Foreign Affairs and the Government on all aspects of foreign policy. Its mission is to promote the interests of Ireland within the European Union and in the wider world and to coordinate Ireland's response to international developments. It helps to promote trade and investment through its network of Missions abroad.

Enterprise Ireland
www.enterprise-ireland.com
Enterprise Ireland is the national organisation with responsibility for accelerating Ireland's national and regional development by helping Irish companies to develop and compete so that they can grow profitably in world markets. Enterprise Ireland's clients are primarily manufacturing and internationally traded services companies employing 10 or more, and new enterprises with the potential to grow rapidly. Enterprise Ireland focuses its resources on companies that are characterised by high levels of ambition, innovation and commitment to international growth.

ESB International
www.esbi.ie
ESB International is one of the world's most successful and well-respected electricity contracting and engineering consultancy organisations. It is also a leading international project developer, owner and independent operator of power generation and distribution assets around the world. With over 25 years' international experience across 90 countries, ESB International offers clients and partners a substantial proven track record across a broad range of utility services in power system development, asset investment and facility management. ESB International is a wholly owned subsidiary of ESB, Ireland's national electricity utility.

FreightWatch Group Ltd
A logistics security consultancy pioneering the development and implementation of customised, quality and cost-effective global logistics security solutions for manufacturers, third-party logistics service providers and insurers in order to prevent the theft of high value at-risk product in transit. With its headquarters in Dublin, Ireland, FreightWatch Group has wholly-owned FreightWatch subsidaries in Ireland, USA, Mexico, the United Kingdom, the Netherlands and Malaysia. FreightWatch provides a suite of seven core services - Customer Risk Profile, Risk Management Escorts, Security Awareness Training, Consultancy/ Operational Reports, Logistics Security Officers, Secure Distribution and Pre-Employment Checks - which provide a significant value proposition for clients in being preventative, proactive and corrective in reducing symptoms of loss across the logistics industry.

IDA Ireland
www.idaireland.com

IDA Ireland has national responsibility for securing new investment from overseas in manufacturing and international services sectors and for encouraging existing foreign enterprises in Ireland to expand their businesses. The businesses that IDA Ireland seeks to win are internationally-mobile projects that can operate competitively and profitably from Ireland, covering a range of sectors such as electronics, pharmaceuticals and healthcare, engineering and international and financial services. IDA Ireland markets Ireland as an attractive location for overseas investment through its network of offices abroad, emphasising the stability and growing competitiveness of the Irish economy, the favourable tax regime, financial incentives, the skills base and Ireland's active participation in Europe.

Intuition
www.intuition.com

Intuition is a leading provider of electronic learning. The company offers a unique combination of content, platform and advisory services to an international client base. Intuition's traditional core market is the financial market sector and the company has recently evolved to encompass the medical and 3rd level sectors. Intuition is headquartered in Dublin, Ireland with offices in London, New York, Hong Kong and Germany.

IONA Technologies PLC
www.iona.com

Headquartered in Dublin, Ireland, with over 30 offices, 800 employees and 4,500 customers worldwide, and turnover of US$181 million (2001), IONA is the leading e-Business platform provider for web services integration. For the last 10 years, we have delivered standards-based solutions to solve the most difficult integration problems, so our customers can make better decisions and run their businesses more efficiently.

MEI-RELSA
www.mei.ie

MEI-RELSA is the Association of Recognised English Language Schools in Ireland. Its members are regulated by the Irish Department of Education. Functions of the association include cooperative marketing, representation at industry and government level, education and training of English language teachers and the preservation and development of Ireland's reputation as the quality location for learning English.

Naval Service
www.military.ie/naval/

The vision of the Naval Service is to be seen and acknowledged nationally and internationally as flexible, impartial, multi-skilled, well-trained, highly motivated and professional maritime service that is responsive to national needs, its legal obligations and the requirements of all its customers. It provides the maritime element of the State's Defence forces and has a general responsibility to meet contingent and actual maritime defence requirements. It is the State's principal sea-going agency and is tasked with a variety of defence and other roles. Its vessels carry unique characteristics as an expression of State sovereignty and political will at sea and in furthering policy objectives in the international maritime domain.

Ireland

Shanahan Engineering Ltd
www.shanahaneng.ie
Shanahan Engineering is a
leading engineering service
company providing project &
construction management,
commissioning, and operations &
maintenance services to the power
generation, oil & gas and
industrial process sectors. The
company has operated in over 50
countries to date and in 2001
opened its Japan office to expand
business in the region further.

Tourism Ireland
www.tourismireland.com
Tourism Ireland was established
under the framework of the
Belfast Agreement of Good
Friday 1998. Its goals are to
promote increased tourism to
the island of Ireland and to
support the industry in
Northern Ireland to reach its
potential. Jointly funded by the
two governments, North and
South, Tourism Ireland has
been fully operational since the
beginning of 2002, when it
launched an extensive
programme to market the entire
island of Ireland overseas as a
tourism destination. Tourism
Ireland, in addition to its
primary strategic destination
marketing role, also undertakes
regional/product marketing and
promotional activities on behalf
of Bord Fáilte and the Northern
Ireland Tourist Board, through
its network of 18 overseas
offices.

RIGHT: The ship's radar display

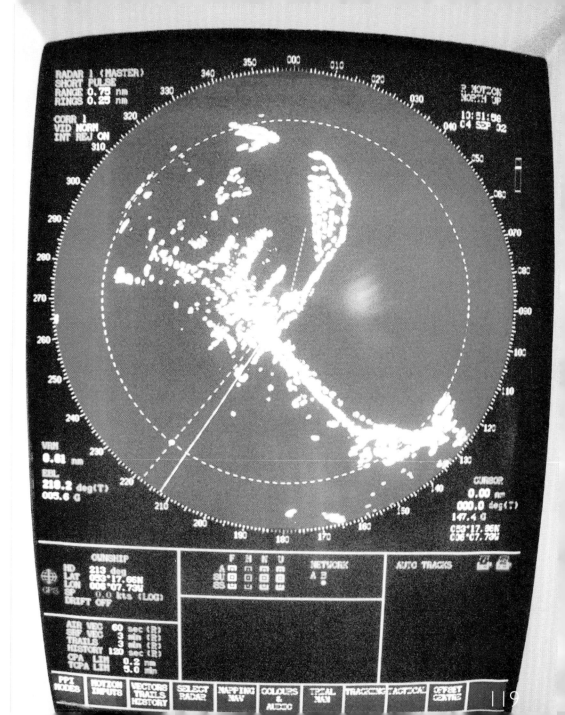

Oak Tree Press

Oak Tree Press is Ireland's leading business book publisher,
with over 150 titles in business, management, law, finance
and human resources.

Oak Tree Press has also developed pre-start-up, start-up,
growth and support content platforms, to meet different user needs.
The platforms include publications, websites, software, training and
consultancy, and certification and are in use in Ireland, UK,
Scandinavia, USA and Eastern Europe.

For further information, contact:
OAK TREE PRESS
19 Rutland Street, Cork, Ireland
T: + 353 21 431 3855 **F:** + 353 21 431 3496
E: info@oaktreepress.com
W: www.oaktreepress.com

www.oaktreepress.com